Just Inside My Head

Just Inside My Head

To Sheelagh - Brian —
It was lovely to meet you
both again!

Jay - Paul

April 2011

Jay Norris

Published by Jay Norris

ISBN 978-0-9566684-0-0

Prepared and printed by:

York Publishing Services Ltd
64 Hallfield Road
Layerthorpe
York YO31 7ZQ
Tel: 01904 431213

Website: www.yps-publishing.co.uk

DEDICATED TO ALL THE BRICKS, BOTH PAST AND PRESENT,
IN MY WALL OF FRIENDSHIP

Packing my bag with useless bits of paper
I wonder, when the last word has been said,
If I'd prefer to find each word was thudding
Not round the school, but just inside my head.

Charles Causley "SCHOOL AT FOUR O'CLOCK"

Contents

I couldn't have done this without:

Richard, a superb editor who knew just how to keep my exclamation marks in order!

Paul, whose patience has been sorely tried by my struggles with the laptop, but who has kept me going when all seemed lost.

Jan, the best and nicest telephone adviser in the whole world.

Mike, a never failing source of artistic support.

Charlie, a writer's best friend, with a Bardic eye for a title.

Giles, as ever, always full of good ideas.

The Cathi/Clare combination at YPS, whose expertise has produced the finished article.

And the inspiration of Charles Causley's poetry

MANY, MANY, THANKS TO YOU ALL

Chapter 1

I've always loved verse, and that was really down to my mother. When "Buddy" was young, she was expected to master the social skills that were a very important part of affluent middle-class family life, in late Victorian times. As well as being generally charming and dressing well, a young lady would usually learn to play something or, if she was lucky enough to have a good voice, she could sing. The great popularity of music hall songs and well-loved romantic ballads, made this a very desirable option and almost every drawing room boasted a piano.

Passionately fond of horses, and with absolutely no musical ability, Buddy had a very real problem. Although she always vehemently denied it, she was completely tone deaf, and was only able recognise the National Anthem because everyone stood up. Over the years, she never seemed to realise the effect this had on her hymn-singing in church. She always sang a completely different, totally unrecognisable tune of her own invention, loudly and enthusiastically. She often got very funny looks from the rest of the congregation, and as soon as I was old enough to be embarrassed, I used to pretend that I was with the person on the other side of me in the pew.

Luckily, there was an acceptable social skill that attracted her. Recitation. She took to it with great gusto. Her special party-piece, Robert Browning's "The Pied Piper of Hamelin", had two advantages. It was suitably dramatic and it was long. It was also satisfactory from the audience's point of view. There was never time for an encore! She loved reciting it. Once she got started there was no stopping her, and I knew most of the poem by the time I was five.

I particularly liked the bits about the rats and their eccentric behaviour. Why did they make their nests inside men's Sunday hats? I hoped there weren't any baby rats left in there, when Sunday came and the men put on their hats. Buddy rather favoured the descriptions of the Pied Piper himself, his 'queer long coat', his bright blue eyes and his 'lips where smiles went out and in'. Her voice always softened, (and so did mine), when she reached those lines. I used to feel sorry for the one boy who got left behind, but I felt he should have tried a bit harder to keep up. It was a wonderful story.

Buddy also had a supporting repertoire of shorter pieces. "The Lost Baby" and "Little Jim", were suitably heartrending, both protagonists succumbing fairly early to adverse circumstances. Baby finished up alone on a snowdrift, finding an easy way to join her mother in "the shining sky", whereas Jim's deathbed was enlivened by weeping parents, taking comfort in the news that, "The angels do so smile and beckon little Jim!". Gloom and doom all the way.

Even the weather always sounded suitably depressing. Baby "wandered out one dismal day" and for Jim "The night was dark and stormy / The wind was howling wild," Not a barrel of laughs, but these poems were immensely popular and, satisfyingly, spoke of uncomfortable happenings, well outside the safe world of the drawing room. They also attempted to make acceptable, the day to day reality of losing one or more children, pragmatically trying to show death as a 'happy-ever-after' ending to a young life. I really enjoyed reciting them with Buddy, making very sure that I exactly copied her tone. She was the expert.

My favourite in her repertoire was rather more cheerful. "Ask Mama" was Victorian fun. Mr Friendly, "a bachelor squire", decides to "comfort his days by taking a wife". (A slightly chauvinistic approach to marriage!)

"The very next day to fair Fanny's amazement
She saw him approach as she stood at the casement,
And he very soon gave her to know his desire,
That she should become the dear wife of the squire."

She is completely taken aback. So, "to give the proposal the greater éclat", she coyly declares that he must "Ask Mama!". It's all downhill from then on, for poor Fanny. Mr Friendly does as she suggests and comes back with the good news that Mama has consented. Her brief moment of delight is shattered when he goes on to say how very pleased he is that she likes her 'new Papa'. As a little girl, I thought the final lines were wonderful:

"The very next time she'd a chance, you may guess,
Not to say 'Ask Mama!', but at once to say.....YES! "

We would collapse with laughter.

Buddy, née Dorothy Florence Higgs, was a remarkable woman. She had trained as a nurse at Bart's, much against her father's wishes. He believed that a daughter should stay at home, until she found a socially acceptable husband, with a good income. Her younger sister, Maudie, had done just that, marrying a second cousin, Frank, who was a successful dental surgeon. Buddy was always extremely energetic, and had very thick, long, chestnut brown hair. She was full of life and popular, and her poetry recitals brought her many admirers. Chief among these was dashing Sid Ives, and they were more or less, engaged. He had a very good job, and excellent prospects, with Pol Roger, the champagne firm, but a quarrel had caused a rift in the romance, and she had gone to Bognor, for a few days to think things over. It was there, while she was staying at the family's holiday home, Arundel Villa, that she met my father.

In normal circumstances, their paths would never have crossed. Buddy's father, Alfred Higgs, with bright ginger hair and blue eyes, was a successful business man, proud of his descent from the first speaker of the House of Commons. He was a qualified pharmacist, president of the Thames Valley Pharmaceutical Society, and had a large chemist's shop in Kingston-on-Thames. He had been the youngest magistrate on the local bench, and his house was the first in the town to have electric light and the telephone. His father had been the headmaster of a village school in Berkshire, and Buddy's brothers were both educated at public schools, while she and her sister went to the highly-rated Tiffin's High School for Girls in Kingston.

The Douglases were a completely different cup of tea. They were carriage folk, blue blooded and proud of it, tracing their descent, directly, to Sir James, the Black Douglas, the close friend of Robert the Bruce. The family crest was a bleeding heart, surmounted by a crown, as the Black Douglas had taken the heart of Bruce to the Crusades, to fulfil the king's dying wish. The family motto, 'Jamais Arrière', 'Never Backwards', recalled bravery in battle and service to the Kings of Scotland. William Douglas, a civil engineer from the Borders, and his wife, Elizabeth, had five children, a girl, Mary, followed by four boys, Robert, John, Charles and Arthur. Mary had been a debutante, presented at court to Queen Victoria. I sometimes stayed with her in the school holidays, and I used to admire an early photograph, on the grand piano in the drawing room, in which she looked beautiful and elegant in a magnificent gown, with an ostrich feather headdress. It was said that the Prince of Wales was impressed enough to send her flowers, but, as he was a married man with an eye for a pretty girl, my grandmother returned them.

Two of my father's brothers were clergymen, and the third was a civil engineer. The family was, socially, very well-connected, and their mother, Elizabeth, had been prepared for confirmation by the Archbishop of Canterbury. Robert was her eldest son. He always called her "the little mater", and there was a strong bond of affection between them. He was delicate, having had rheumatic fever when he was young. He was, also, asthmatic, but had been sent away to school at Brighton College, and had become a talented linguist, speaking seven languages, including Russian and Chinese. He had lived for a short while in both Paris and Moscow, but he had never been expected to have a proper job, or to marry.

He was convalescing in Bognor Regis, when, while taking a stroll along the promenade on a very windy day, he had spotted Buddy, swimming alone, in a rough sea. He was intrigued, and managed to find out who she was, and get an introduction to this fearless young lady. When he met her, he fell deeply in love. He courted her passionately, walking up and down outside Bart's hospital, when she went back to London, in the hope that he might see her, much to the amusement of her fellow nurses. She was immensely flattered, and Sid Ives was forgotten in the excitement of her new conquest. Robert was nearly twenty years older than Buddy, but he had a great deal of charm, a lovely voice, and beautiful manners. He proposed to her and she accepted.

Two very important people strongly opposed the marriage. Her father, because Robert had no settled income or, apparently, the energy to pursue an academic career that would earn enough to support a family: and his mother, to whom the news came as a very unpleasant surprise. She was about to lose her favourite son to a nurse, not a socially acceptable career, whose father had a chemist's shop, and was, therefore, 'in trade'. However, they were both over twenty-one, love conquered all, and they married in the church at Mortlake, where Buddy's younger brother, also a chemist, owned and ran 'Stewart's Pharmacy'.

My Aunt Mary once remarked, that it was the wisest thing my father ever did. He gained a young, energetic wife, with all the professional skills needed to nurse him when he was unwell. He proved to be a loving husband, and in the first two years of their marriage, they had two little girls, Margaret and Elizabeth, always called, Peggy and Betty. I came on the scene over seven years later, just seven months after Betty had, quite unexpectedly, died of meningitis, in Great Ormond Street Hospital. They were absolutely devastated. She had been a happy, outgoing little girl, with golden hair and bright blue eyes, and I grew up with a framed picture of her, on the wall over Buddy's bed, entitled 'Angel Betty'. She was the icon of my childhood, and gave me my great love of blue eyes.

I remember my father as kind and gentle, and having a gold pen, as well as the gold pencil that I was, sometimes, allowed to play with. His foreign private pupils came to our house for English lessons in his study, which had a very big desk and books on shelves that went right up to the ceiling. He also occasionally lectured, on a free lance basis, at London University, on the teaching of English to foreigners. For pleasure, he wrote poetry, often in rhymed couplets, and articles for the parish magazine of St Luke's, in Peckham, where his brothers, John and Charles, were vicar and curate. Money was definitely tight, though we had a cook and a parlourmaid, and Buddy occasionally did some private nursing, to help pay the bills.

One April, when the winter he always dreaded was over, returning from lecturing at the university, he got soaked to the skin in a sudden shower of rain, and caught cold. Within days, a cough had turned to pneumonia and pleurisy, and he died on April 29th. I remember being lifted on to the great big bed, and being told to, "Say goodbye to Daddy", and I thought that he felt very hot when he kissed me. He was in his early sixties, the coffers were empty and Buddy had to sell his books to pay the funeral expenses. She was forty-two, Peggy was thirteen and I was five. The family whisked Peggy off to finish her education at a convent, in Bruges, in Belgium, but I was, clearly, too young to be parted from my mother. Strangely, no one seems to have considered the possibility that Buddy would need any long-term financial help. After all, she was a State Registered Nurse, and therefore, perfectly capable of supporting us both, and that was exactly what she proceeded to do.

Chapter 2

Her first appointment, after she was widowed, was as Assistant Matron in a children's convalescent home, in Redhill, in Surrey, so, at least, we had somewhere to live. I remember that the Matron had an adopted little girl, who was very pretty. I once heard Buddy say, enviously, that 'Tinkles', as she was called, would 'look nice in a sack', and I knew that meant that I didn't, so I really envied Tinkles. It was, I realised, a great advantage to be pretty. From there, Buddy became matron of a similar home, for Jewish children, at St Leonard's, on the Sussex coast, where she nearly caused a major religious upset, by trying to snatch the boys' skull caps off, as they went to a service in the synagogue.

St Leonard's was the posh end of Hastings, probably still is, and tourists tended to stay in the little guest houses at the fishing port. The Salvation Army often held summer prayer meetings on the beach there, and they would sing about a free journey to Paradise, that amused Buddy immensely.

"Nothing to pay, no, nothing to pay, from Hastings to glory, there's nothing to pay!"

Finally, when I was nine, she applied for a post as Matron of 'The British Dental Hospital', in south-west London. It was , basically, a clinic for the less well-off, and we would have our own self-contained flat, on the first floor of a large Victorian house, with a big garden. Resident caretakers in the basement, did all the cleaning and gardening, and the dental surgery and the patients' waiting and recovery rooms, were on the ground floor. Buddy was really thrilled when she was appointed, for now we would have our own home again, with our very own kitchen. She had grown tired of the food in various institutions, even though the Matron was always well looked after, with her own maid, and the cook frequently sending up special dishes from the kitchen.

The new appointment turned out well, and it was at about this time when, asking for pocket money, I sang "Buddy, can you spare a dime?", and, as it amused her, I got my reward, and she was 'Buddy' from then on. One unexpected bonus of the new job was that, as the clinic was, 'The British Dental HOSPITAL', theatre ticket agencies constantly offered free seats to the 'nursing staff'. This was called, "papering the house", and they were always the most expensive stalls and boxes, that the agency had been unable to sell. Despite feeling slightly guilty, Buddy took advantage of this largesse, and, for several years, we saw every flop in the West End, absolutely free. It gave me a love of going to the theatre, particularly in the best seats!

The comparatively easy task of running the clinics for the impressively suave, and very charming, male dental surgeons, suited Buddy down to the ground, and I was sent to the nearby, fee-paying, 'Convent of the Holy Family High School for Girls', just around the corner in Tooting Broadway. That turned out pretty well too, for there I met an English teacher to die for. When she was out of earshot, we called Sister du Saint Coeur de Marie, 'Sankey', and she was a superb teacher, who absolutely loved poetry and Shakespeare. She thought they should be enjoyed, studied, and learnt by heart. I was delighted. All that reciting with Buddy, unexpectedly paid off.

I added another poem to my growing repertoire, when my sister, Peggy, learnt 'The Highwayman', by Alfred Noyes for a Guide Badge test. If I heard something in rhyme, often enough, it stuck in my head, and, thereafter, I knew it, word for word, permanently. I loved the romance between the glamorous highwaymen, whose 'boots came up to his thigh', which sounded terribly sexy, and the red- lipped inn keeper's daughter. I hated Tim, the ostler, with his hair 'like mouldy hay', who betrayed the lovers, and the terrible climax, when she dies, as she attempts to warn her sweetheart. The return of their ghosts, to renew their vows, on a winter's night, 'when the wind is in the trees', (even in more modern poems there still seemed to be a comment on the weather), made a really wonderful ending.

Learning by heart, seemed to me to be the most natural thing in the world, and English lessons, with Sankey, were the greatest fun. She introduced us to the Romantic Poets, (we all thought that John Keats was her favourite), the War Poets, (I loved Rupert Brooke), and to the wonders of Shakespeare. We had dramatic readings, in class, of 'The Merchant of Venice', followed closely by 'Julius Caesar'. First Sankey read the play through, and then we all took a part, with everyone always wanting to be Brutus or Mark Anthony. I was in my element, had a trained memory, and absolutely no inhibitions about showing off. I entered into the spirit of English lessons with a bumptious enthusiasm, which, for better or worse, I don't think I've ever lost!

When The British Dental Hospital closed, Buddy became Matron of St Benedict's , a large private nursing home in Nightingale Lane, so that I could stay at the convent school in Tooting, It was a non-resident post, and we lived in various unfurnished flats, in the prestigious roads around Wandsworth Common. I often used to go to St Benedict's after school, and spent a lot of time playing board games with the patients, to keep them amused. A very popular one was called 'Sorry!', and the cheerful apology you had to give, when you knocked your opponent's piece off the board, made it great fun for both players.

I was also expected, as Matron's daughter, to push disabled patients, in their wheelchairs, up to Wandsworth Common, for a change of scenery. I wasn't very big and some of them were very heavy, so, several times, as we went down the rather steep hill, I was afraid that the chair would run away, out of control. I particularly dreaded taking Miss Penny, who had had a stroke, and weighed a ton. She was very impatient if we went too fast, and I had, more or less, decided to let go of the handle, if the worst happened. The bad-tempered woman would then go racing off on her own, though quite what trouble I'd have got into, I didn't dare to think. Buddy liked to move house fairly regularly, and would quickly get bored with wherever we were living at any given moment, so we spent lots of time flat-hunting, and life was never dull.

Years later, after I had left home, she wanted to have a house of her own, so she moved to Enfield, in north London, as one of two nurses in the District Nursing Association. The 'hands on', personal contacts in the community, suited her, and she cycled everywhere. Eventually, she even invested in an auto bike, with a little put-put engine, that made the longer journeys less tiring. She worked very hard, and the patients liked and trusted, cheerful, efficient 'Nurse Douglas'. Having, initially, lied about her age, she was, actually, over seventy by the time she officially left, and took private patients. Retirement meant that she could, finally, claim the state pension that, at the time, was paid at the local Post Office. Buddy had never dared risk someone seeing her there, and spilling the beans about her real age!

Writing verse, of one kind or another turned out to be a natural follow-on to Buddy's poetry sessions. It was, as they say, 'for amusement only'. Back from the USA, where I'd spent time in Oklahoma, Florida and New York, and waiting to go to Teacher Training College, I took a job as 'Customer Liaison Officer' with a large local firm. Maws of Barnet were manufacturing chemists, very proud of the fact that the firm had been established in 1815. In post-war Britain, however, they definitely had huge organisational problems, in both stock control and the delivery of goods. None of the managerial staff had the faintest idea exactly what was wrong, or how to put things right. No-one even knew how to pass the buck, when customers complained, which they frequently did.

Professional 'efficiency experts' had been engaged to identify problem areas and, where possible, to modernise antiquated procedures in the firm's organisation. Inevitably, the result was chaotic and I was employed to smooth the many resulting ruffled feathers. I was kept very busy inventing tactful excuses, either on the phone or by dictating letters of abject apology, to Betty, my very efficient personal secretary. After one particularly stressful day, when Betty was clearly getting sick of apologising for one thing or another, I wrote a little verse to cheer her up.

AN ODE TO THE EFFICIENCY EXPERTS

Come let us greet with loud applause
The Iron Men who rule at Maws!
For every day, with ponderous frown,
They pace the office up and down,
While little clerks grow faint with terror.
(Good heavens! Have I made an error?)

And every minute comes the moan
Of voices on the telephone.
Yes? What's the problem? Sorry, sir,
To make your truss will take a year.
You need a belt? I must reply
These items are in short supply!

The typist hammers her machine,
(You'll only get on if you're keen!)
For this is a progressive firm,
Their policies are all long-term.
Why, since the time of Waterloo
Their very best they've tried to do!

Is there a shortage, someone bleats,
Of anti-colic welfare teats?
And why, the angry chemist asks,
Can't they dispatch my thermos flasks?
Sssh, whisper it behind closed doors....
Efficiency has come to Maws!

Keeping Betty as a friend, at the start of the new term I resigned from customer liaison at Maws, and went to train, for what I hoped might be a more satisfying career, as a teacher. The course I had chosen was called 'ENGLISH with DRAMA', at Trent Park College in Cockfosters.

Going back to studying again kept me too busy to write anything, other than interminable essays, about this and that, in subjects like Psychology and the Philosophy of Education. I was amazed at what a load of rubbish much of it seemed to be, but I was careful to keep such feelings to myself. Phrases like 'sibling rivalry' fascinated me, and threw some light on why my sister and I found each other so irritating. It would have been an interesting area to explore in verse, but I had neither the time nor the energy to spare.

I was really looking forward to my first teaching practice, when I hoped to give the kind of English lessons that had inspired me at school, and I was excited by the prospect of opening doors into an enchanted world. I knew absolutely nothing about state schools, but, if I gave it any consideration at all, I probably expected them to be like the Holy Family Convent High School for Girls.

When I heard where my introduction to the teaching profession was to take place, I drove down to take a look at the outside of the school. It was the weekend and, the street in Edmonton, on the outskirts of London, was almost completely deserted. The building was red-brick Victorian, with entrances labelled BOYS and GIRLS, and surrounded by a tarmac playground. It had been an old elementary school, and now the Butler Education Act had made it into a new Secondary Modern for, supposedly, less academic pupils.

An examination at eleven-plus, decided which children went there. The quality and commitment of the staff would decide how successful the experiment in selection would be. I wanted to help in any way I could, so the lessons must buzz with exciting ideas, including, of course, poetry. Reality came when we arrived on the following Thursday to begin our first teaching practice.

Joyce, a fellow student specialising in music, and I, got to the school full of trepidation, and were ushered into the headmaster's study. He looked very hang-dog and was keen to 'put us in the picture' of what to expect. Clearly, not a lot. He particularly wanted to warn us against trying out any of those new-fangled ideas that college might have put into our silly little heads. He showed us a long list of the names of teaching staff who had abandoned the struggle and had left the school after, in some instances, less than one term. We would be lucky to survive, but he wished us well. I almost expected him to say he'd keep his fingers crossed for us. In fact, we both spent four fascinating weeks in his school, Joyce with her Music, and me with my English, including poetry!

By the end of the four weeks, when we went to his study to say goodbye, and thank him for having us, he had obviously heard about our rash forays into such previously unheard-of experiences of culture for the pupils. He spoke quite kindly, letting us know that he considered that we had been very lucky to 'get away' with the rather revolutionary ideas we had tried. He even admitted to having been amazed that, introducing 'poetry' into a lesson with fourteen year olds had not resulted in major disruption in the classroom. Yet he gave us both an 'A', and I still have a copy of the testimonial from college, in which he is recorded as commenting, "She would make a good head of a primary school". I still haven't worked out whether, as a secondary headmaster, he meant it as a compliment or not!

Chapter 3

Back at Trent Park, it was nearly the end of our first term and I was on the editorial committee of the college magazine. I had been writing the Gossip Column, under the pen name of Betty Bawd, and I needed a special message for Christmas. I couldn't resist the temptation of writing in verse.....

A SEASONAL MESSAGE

Pack your brush and comb, my dear,
The Christmas Holidays are here!
You're thinking you'll have lots of fun
Now that the term its course has run.
Away with dreams of carefree youth,
You have to face this awful truth......
While others, at parties, seek elation,
You'll read BOOKS ON EDUCATION!
B.B.

I really enjoyed college and never found it too stressful, even though, in my final year, I was President of the Students' Union. There were so many new things to do, that I hardly knew where to start. An annual film had to be made and thanks to Dennis, an art student who proved to be a natural cameraman, enthusiastically assisted by his girl friend, Pam, we successfully completed a drama called 'No Other Heaven'.

The whole story hinged on using the background of Trent Park to the best advantage. It was spring, and I wrote a story of 'rags to riches', in which the little heiress to the house fell for the son of one of the gardeners. All rather predictable, but we found two very good children and they looked darling, in among Trent's superb show of daffodils. However, when we tried to add the dialogue, there were real problems. I had written a scene in which the little girl overhears the servants talking, and realises, with horror, that her parents have been killed in a car crash. We had a movie camera and we had a tape recorder, but there was no synchronisation between the two. After trying every possible option, Dennis, as camera man, suggested that he would always make sure that you couldn't see anyone's lips when they were speaking. It was a great idea and it worked, so with a sigh of relief, we managed to finish the film.

I thoroughly enjoyed the practical side of the drama course and it was wonderful to be acting again. I was lucky enough to play some comedy roles that were fun, and not too demanding, like Lady Caroline in "The Admirable Crichton", and the French maid in a farce called "Nine till Five". Our group included Gwen, who had delightful bridge-playing parents, nicknamed by us, Noel and Gertie, plus a dear little red-haired sister called Flicky. They became our close friends, and Gwen played 'Ratty' to my 'Toad', in a college Open Day production of a scene from 'Toad of Toad Hall', a play that has come into my life over and over again!

With my training over, and the final exam hurdle safely behind me, the next thing was to start my career as a teacher of English and Drama. As soon as I would be earning a salary, Ernest and I could buy our first house, and, thanks to good college grades, I quickly got a job. It was as an assistant teacher of English, at a new Secondary Modern school in East Herts.

In 1952, Cheshunt was a little country town on the northern outskirts of London. It was quite prosperous, with plenty of unskilled jobs in the largest area under glass in Europe. Firms like Rochfords, grew tomatoes and pot plants for the retail market, while a grocery outlet, 'Tesco' (named after the founder's wife, Tessa Cohen), set up headquarters in

Delamare Road. Two quite extensive council estates had been built, one for local people at Bury Green, and one to house families, displaced by the wartime bombing of London.

After some enthusiastic house-hunting, and the chatting-up of local agents, we found just what we wanted, a three-bedroom, post-war semi, at the reasonable, 'controlled', price of £2,500. It was set at the end of quiet Pine Close, just off the A10, Great Cambridge Road, and about a ten minute walk from my new school. A short bike ride would take Ernest to Cheshunt railway station every morning, for his journey to Liverpool Street, and there were plenty of good primary schools for Paul.

The house had quite a big garden, a first for Ernest, who came to enjoy working in it at weekends. The previous owners had made a vegetable plot, and there were fruit trees, and a well-kept lawn for Paul to play on. We added a lean-to conservatory for entertaining, and filled it with rubber plants and monstera, large house plants, that we bought from a nearby nursery called, by a strange coincidence, 'Ernest Paul'! One very real bonus was that our garden backed on to the country training ground of Tottenham Hotspur Football Club, so we thought that no houses could ever be built there, to spoil the country views. We gave our new home a name, "Wits End", and we were to stay there, very happily, for the next seventeen years!

Cheshunt County Secondary School, to give it its full name, was exactly what I had hoped for. In 1952, it was still being built, and for the first two years we taught to the intrusive scream of the circular saws, outside ground floor classrooms. The building was constructed from concrete, steel and glass, the post-war architectural 'new look' for schools. (They built toothbrush factories that looked just the same.) Large classrooms, each with a number, led off the bottom main corridor, and, at intervals, there were staircases, each with two classrooms at the top. For the first few years I taught in Room 9, on the ground floor, and I grew very fond of it.

The 'Admin Block' was in a separate, adjoining building and included a magnificent school hall, that could seat an audience of over five hundred. It had a huge stage, with a thirty-five foot proscenium opening, as wide as many in West End theatres. Double doors led into the hall, and there was an impressive vestibule area. From here, a staircase went up to the balcony and the very big staff room.

Another door opened onto a narrow corridor, along which were set the Head's study, and the school secretary's office, where the dinner money was counted every Monday morning. Rooms for the Senior Mistress and the Deputy Head, the Medical Room, with the school nurse in attendance, and the staff washrooms, completed the picture. I was surprised at how many non-teaching jobs there were in a school, and how important they seemed to be. It certainly wasn't like that at the Holy Family Convent, where, as it was an enclosed order, no men were ever allowed past the front parlour.

On the front drive, opposite the hard tennis courts, that became netball courts in the winter, the caretaker had a nice bungalow with its own garden. There were lots of parking spaces for staff and visitors, in front of the school building, and, by the side of the A10, there was a five acre sports field, for rugby, soccer and athletics. We thought we were very lucky.

The new full-time staff of about 54, had more men than women. There was a mixture of experienced and newly qualified teachers, the youngest in their early twenties. Some of the older ones were nearing retirement and had taught in local elementary schools, where the leaving age had been 14, and from which the pupils had been transferred to form the new school's student body. Many of the younger staff were, like me, fresh out of college, excited at the thought of making a success of their teaching careers, and welcoming the chance to try out all those new-fangled ideas. It was easy to settle down in such pleasant surroundings, and I stayed for thirty years, finally retiring, from there, as Senior Mistress!

There was a meeting of the whole staff, two days before term began. We were given our personal timetables and a chance to look each other over. I had not known quite what to wear and, much to Ernest's amusement, tried out several alternative outfits, before settling on a blouse and skirt, in an unobtrusive combination of navy and white. We were asked to stand up, one after another, to be identified, and

I particularly liked the look of Sue, who was to teach French, and an attractive young chap called Keith, who was in the Maths department. These first impressions proved to be spot on.

Keith became the dearest friend I have ever had. Very sadly, he died of a heart attack in 1974, just as we started the week's run of "A Midsummer Night's Dream". He was only 47, and I still miss him, while Sue and I have remained close friends for fifty-eight years. Both of them cheerfully took part in lots of future fun, and I wrote masses of rhymed couplets either for entertainments at school, or for birthday 'car rallies', on July 14th at 'Wits End'.

Over the years, I found it impossible to resist the opportunities that staff parties offered for tongue-in-cheek critical comment on minor irritations at school. It was easy to offer gentle rebukes in rhyme, that, made openly, would have been quite unacceptable.

Several years later, when the secondary modern experiment had ended in Hertfordshire, the school changed its name. It became a comprehensive, to be known as 'Riversmead'. We were all still full of beans and everything seemed to be going well, when a new member of staff appeared, straight out of college. He seemed pleasant enough, keen and well-meaning, but he had very clear ideas about how a new comprehensive school ought to be run, and he felt he should tell us where, in his opinion, we were going wrong.

In the staff room, at lunchtime or after school, he would offer a great deal of unsolicited advice, to anyone who would listen. He said he felt that some of our more difficult pupils could be dealt with in a totally different way. There was, he suggested, a radical new approach to the relationship between teachers and pupils. It was based on the important psychological needs of adolescent boys and girls. We should try it. We needed to unbend.

He was basically a nice chap, in his twenties, and we were a young staff, but, by then, in our thirties. (Actually, we had thought that we were reasonably unbent!) People all listened politely, hoping that time, and daily brushes with adolescent boys and girls, would show him the error of his ways, but he kept on and on. He was certainly having some discipline problems, as the noise in the corridor outside his room suggested, but it was awkward to intervene until something untoward happened. At the end of his first term, came the staff Christmas Party and, of course, the entertainment included, a not-too-subtle monologue, tailor-made, especially for him!

THE TALE OF RUPERT BEAR

Now Rupert's mother said one day,
"It's time you learnt to work, not play,
And I am really certain, dear,
That you should choose a good career.
For, if you follow my advice,
You'll find that teaching's very nice!"
So, Rupert, seeking after knowledge,
Spent three years at a Training College,
And then, to meet the country's need,
He went to teach at Shiversread,
A 'modern' school, which you will see,
Was changing comprehensively.

A special course had Rupert done,
For general subjects, with Form One,
To read, and spell, and count and write,
For Rupert was so erudite.
The staff, now ageing, saw the truth,
They can't compete with Rupert's youth.
Their old ideas could not survive,
(For he was under twenty-five!)
Yes, good at work and sport was he,
And full of personality.
Both blithe and gay, he must succeed
At bringing life to Shiversread.

The first day caused the class to stare,
Their teacher was a little bear,
And very shortly, we shall see,
There's fun in store for 1RB!
Success was now within his reach.
At College, where he'd learnt to teach,
They'd told him of a splendid ruse
The classroom desks you never use,
For work must not become a bore.
Get out on visits by the score.
Don't play the hawk, but be a dove,
A teacher all the pupils love!

So, with these maxims in his mind,
Young Rupert Bear was very kind,
He never spoke an angry word,
Though what he said was seldom heard,
And all his classes, as a rule,
Were audible throughout the school.
When told of this he was elated,
"My lessons have communicated,
The class all know that I'm their buddy,
Not just another fuddy-duddy!"
He understood their every need,
This bright young star of Shiversread.

When in the staff room, he would speak
Of new ideas he'd tried that week.
"You older ones, your ways should mend,
Look on each pupil as a friend!"
(One member of the staff was heard
To say a rather naughty word,
And make a gesture with his hand,
That Rupert did not understand.)
At all the meetings of the staff
He'd tell them, with his jolly laugh,
That if they'd only take his cue,
They soon would solve their problems too.

At last, one kinder than the rest,
Said, "Mr Bear, I know what's best,
I'm sure, with all that special knowledge,
You ought to teach in Training College!"
So Rupert went and saw the Head,
Who listened carefully, then said,
"Yes, Mr Bear, to me it's plain,
I think their loss would be our gain.
I'm not the one to stop you leaving."
But Rupert saw that he was grieving.
"Their loss our gain...", and then he frowned.
........The Head had said it wrong way round!!

At the end, I looked across at our very own Rupert Bear, who was smiling bravely, and, perhaps it was wishful thinking on my part, but he seemed to be much less irritating thereafter. Interestingly, several friends from other schools asked to borrow the rhyme, to use at their parties, so maybe we weren't the only ones with a problem!

Chapter 4

Back in 1952, well before the Rupert Bear years, we were all just settling down in Cheshunt County Secondary Modern School. The new intake of pupils, who arrived in September, at the same time as I did, spent their first three terms in the old Boys' Brigade huts, on the edge of the playing fields. There simply wasn't room for them yet, in the new building. Two of the older teachers guided them through the trauma of starting secondary education in a big school, after the past protected life of small local primaries.

An additional stress at that time was the effect of the 1944 Butler Act. The much desired entry to the well-established, sought-after, local grammar schools was limited, in East Herts., to the children in the top eight-and-a-half percent of the 11plus examinations. Many parents were extremely disappointed when their offspring were 'selected' for a place at the new Secondary Modern school, and these unfortunates were considered to have 'failed', rather than to have been 'chosen' for a less academic education. Naturally, this did not help such children, particularly the brighter ones, to settle down happily in the new regime. Local feelings ran quite high, at the perceived unfairness of the selection process.

Amazingly, in the 1952 intake, there were two new eleven year old pupils, Janice and Harry, who were, much later, to become long-term, close friends. They both did extremely well at school and have been very successful in their chosen careers. Janice, (happily married to Mike, with three children, Ruth, Clare and Paul), became a superb teacher of handicapped pupils, and Harry, (changing his name to Cliff Richard), became a world famous pop-star!

The very first Christmas staff party, in 1952, was great fun. As the only, so-called, teacher of drama, I was asked by the organising committee to arrange some kind of entertainment. There would be a formal sit-down dinner, and, to allow that to be digested, there would be a break before the dancing started. Filling that gap in the proceedings was to be my responsibility. It was with considerable trepidation that I put up a list in the staff room asking anyone willing to perform, to sign. To my great relief there seemed to be enough volunteers, to put on a reasonably varied programme.

A rather jolly young scientist offered to do a mime, and Keith signed up to do 'The Laughing Policeman'. Sue, with Jill from Needlework, offered to join in too, so it seemed a good moment to try and write something that we could be in together.

I can only remember the first and last verses of what I wrote. The three of us wore various school uniforms. Jill, who was tall, looked very smart in green, as worn by the local grammar school. Sue, very professional in black and white, seemed every inch a representative of the technical college, and I was a total mess, in crumpled navy blue, our own school colour. I had a navy beret, not the most flattering headgear, pulled right down to my eyebrows. We began in unison.

"We all started off in the primary school,
But intelligence tests at eleven did rule.

(Jill) *That I'm clever,* (Sue) *I'm useful,* (Me) *And I'm just a fool,*
(Jill) *So I'm Grammar,*
(Sue) *I'm Tech,*
(Me) *And I'm Secondary Mod.*

The final verse was, fairly predictably, geared for a laugh.

(Jill and Sue) *Our future employment is easy to see,* (Jill) *I'll teach,* (Sue) *And I'll type,* (Jill & Sue) *And we'll take GCE,*

(Here I had to pull my beret into what, I hoped, was a sexy slant)

(Me) *But I bet you can't guess what'll happen to me?????*

(Jill) *For I'm Grammar, (Sue) I'm Tech,*
(Me, meaningfully!) *And I'm Secondary Mod* !!!!!

We were greeted by gales of laughter and we were delighted. Of course, I'd had the best part, but Sue and Jill were kind-hearted, and didn't seem to grudge me the role. Perhaps they thought that, after all, I had written it!

For the three of us, it was the first of several very successful staff party collaborations. Usefully, I had learnt that comic verse and school events, could go quite easily together, and that seemed to augur well for the future.

Very pleasingly, the rest of the entertainment at that staff party was also extremely successful. The young science teacher's mime, of a totally inept man sewing on a button with a very long piece of thread, was original and side-splitting. Keith brought the house down with a wonderful lip-synch to a recording of 'The Laughing Policeman'. He was, I noted, every bit as talented as I knew he would be. We danced the Charleston together later that evening and he was much better at it than I was. Ernest really enjoyed the party and clearly liked the staff. My new career was turning out very well for all concerned.

Life in the classroom proved to be rather more challenging, to say the least. On entry, the children had taken the school's own tests in English and Maths, and, in the light of these results, they had been put into general ability streams, called Upper, Middle and Lower, A, B and C. Of course, there were bound to be some mistakes, and these had to be put right before any damage was done, one way or the other.

One example was Harry, who was extremely bright. He had been the top boy at his primary school, and was expected to 'pass' for the grammar school. Instead, to everyone's great surprise, he was sent to the newly opened Secondary Modern, where he landed up, inappropriately, in a low ability group. Fortunately, the error was quickly spotted, and Harry was immediately promoted to join Janice in the top stream, so all was well.

Like Miss Jean Brodie's girls, they were our crème de la crème, our pride and joy, so, when I saw 'U2A English', on my new timetable in 1953, I was over the moon. They were to come to Room 9, five times each week, and the lessons were to last for forty-five minutes. The English syllabus was quite flexible, so there would be plenty of time for some choral-speaking and I thought I might even try out some practical classroom drama, and so it turned out!

They were a pleasure to teach, and, when I started a dramatic society that met outside school hours, quite a number of them joined. Brian and John, Frances and Anita, plus Janice and Harry, to name but a few, and over the next four years, they were the mainstay of every school production. We won several local drama festivals with one-act Chinese plays. Harry was often the hero and Janice the heroine, one, or both of them, usually drowning in the lake, or perishing in a vat of molten metal.

By 1955, instead of little one-act productions, we graduated to an impressively staged version of A.A.Milne's, 'Toad of Toad Hall', as the Christmas play. Ken, a wonderfully talented young art teacher, designed and painted the best sets I had ever seen in a school. To his surprise, though not to mine, he also turned out to be brilliant at stage make-up. Brian, who made an impressive Badger, looked exactly like one, and John, a lovable Mole, was transformed into a little furry creature before our very eyes. He even managed to make sweet little Janice look mean and aggressive, as the Chief Weasel. Keith, who was keen on photography, and spent a lot of his salary on cameras with huge lenses, took amazingly professional pictures to display in the vestibule. It was a very good team.

I had typecast Harry as kind, reliable Ratty, but problems arose as soon as I told him that there were some jolly songs to learn. It seemed that he was sorry, but he simply couldn't sing. I told him that that was rubbish. Everyone could sing, (I didn't mention Buddy and the hymns!). It was either do the songs, or lose a very good part to someone else, and after a minute's thought, he decided he would give it a go. His solo, 'All among the backwaters', turned into a real show stopper. Looking very rakish in his sailor hat, he would elegantly twirl the lovely long rat's tail on the hired costume, and get a well-deserved round of applause from the audience. His singing has never looked back!

That year the staff party came when I was still very busy. The play rehearsals for 'Toad', just day to day English marking, and running a home for Ernest and Paul, were extremely time consuming. I was expecting a baby in the following May, so there were arrangements to be made for a supply teacher, for when I took the six weeks of paid maternity leave that the LEA allowed We couldn't afford for me to stay at home, and I, quite definitely, didn't want to.

Upper 2A had, by now, become U4A and I was their form teacher in Room 9. They were to be the school's first real exam Fifth Form and most of them would stay on after they could have left at 15, to take O level GCE. It was a really exciting prospect and I wanted to be a part of it. For the Christmas party entertainment, I turned to parody, which was considerably quicker to write. I pinched Gilbert and Sullivan's 'Mikado' song "Three Little Girls", one of whom was Ken, in a kimono, with knitting needles stuck in the back of his hair, but I can only remember this:

"Three little maids who all unwary,
came to a modern secondary..."

Whatever it was, it went down well. Keith did a superb lip-synch of 'The Song of the Flea', with lots of attempted scratching, which nearly brought the house down, and everyone had a very good time doing the 'Gay Gordons' at the dancing later in the evening. We all looked forward to a great year in '56.

The twelve months till the following Christmas went by in a flash, So much happened. A bouncing baby boy, James Douglas, duly arrived on May 10th. Ernest had suggested 'Peter', pointing out that we already had a 'Paul', however, at the time, I taught a difficult boy with that name, and I certainly didn't want to have a permanent reminder of him.

The December play, 'A Christmas Carol', was a huge success, starring the now very experienced, Brian, Harry and Janice, as Scrooge and the

Cratchits respectively. They were very good, and with Ken's wonderful sets, the whole thing was first class. We had hired the Victorian costumes, and the boys absolutely loved the 'drainpipe' trousers, which certainly looked very smart. Apparently, they were fashionable with the teddy boys, and, in the Green Room, Harry did a brilliant impersonation of the newly popular, Elvis Presley, waggling hips and singing "Heartbreak Hotel".

Though the new fifth form seemed to be doing well, there had been several administrative hiccups in the school year. The fabric of the building was showing unexpected signs of wear and tear, the canteen supervisor had left, and minor thefts of dinner tickets were causing concern. Nothing too serious, but, nevertheless, a worrying trend in the new school, for the three in charge, the fairly well-paid Head, Deputy Head and Senior Mistress. It was a situation made to measure for a gentle parody of "A policeman's lot is not a happy one". With the Head of Music at the piano, Keith, Ken and I, wearing academic gowns, complete with hoods, sang it.

A LIFE OF HEADSHIP

We are here in charge of lots of lads and lasses,
With net curtains in the rooms in which we sit,
Though our salaries are in the upper classes,
And we're capable, industrious and fit.
Yet beneath our gowns our hearts are really breaking,
Though the battle for promotion we have won,
For a friendly smile we're absolutely aching,
A life of headship's not a happy one......happy one,
With those extra little extras to be done, to be done,
A life of headship's not a happy one.

There's a medical inspection due tomorrow,
And a BCG for third years in the week,
There's some children feeling sick, and to our sorrow,
The lavatory system's sprung a leak.
There is someone eating dinner without paying,
And the canteen staff are leaving one by one,
Is it really any wonder that we're saying,
A life of headship's not a happy one......happy one,
With those new part-time timetables to be done, to be done,
A life of headship's not a happy one.

Seven staff are out, protesting at a rally,
And another two have slipped a spinal disc,
Our school journey money total doesn't tally,
And we hear the library ceiling is at risk.
There's a letter from the Min of Ed that's saying
That a school inspection's due to start in June,
You can bet your bottom dollar that we're praying
We'll all be getting other jobs quite soon!
For, although we get more money, we have very little fun,
A life of headship's not a happy one, happy one!

I was relieved, at the end, to see that the Head and his team, seemed to have enjoyed the rhyme, otherwise we might have lost our precious non-teaching free periods in the future.

Chapter 5

After Christmas, I began to increase the pressure on our very first GCSE 'O Level' fifth form, to encourage them to show their paces in the coming summer exams. I was very conscious that, if they failed English Language and Literature, I would feel it was my fault. They had made a very good start and, in Language their true ability showed. They were intelligent and quickly got the hang of précis and essay writing. Most of the class seemed to find parsing and analysis reasonably straightforward, and could spell quite well.

Literature was fun, but I wondered if that would be enough. There were so many tempting things to do that didn't include swotting for an exam. Associated Boards had an interesting syllabus, including Emily Bronte's 'Wuthering Heights', which it had been wonderful to read together. (We could all see that Harry was very taken with the character of Heathcliff.) The poetry anthology was very attractive, with D.H.Lawrence's, 'Snake', and Coleridge's 'Kublai Khan', and, remembering how much I had enjoyed it, I had chosen 'Julius Caesar' as the set play. But, of course, just to like the books wouldn't be enough, they had to be studied, with exam questions in mind.

We read Julius Caesar, dramatically, as I had with Sankey, all those years before, and because, thanks to Hitler, everyone knew about political power struggles, it went down well. Harry's favourite lines were 'Cry havoc, and let slip the dogs of war!' and Norman made us all fall about laughing when, his slightly spotty face crumpling, in an effort to find the words to give an opinion, he said, "It's all right but... it's all them little lines...!"

Janice was really good at English and worked hard, so I was very confident that she would pass easily. So would several of the others, but the interest in Bill Hailey and 'Rock Around the Clock' made me uneasy about some of the boys, which was a huge pity, as they had apparently enjoyed the lessons. Homework, as ever, was a problem. Skiffle groups were springing up all over the place, and Cheshunt seemed to have more than its fair share.

Time outside school was precious, all the more so because wartime austerity was still fresh in the minds of their parents. This new generation had been born at the beginning of the war, so this was, indeed, 'a brave new world'. Many fathers had returned when their children were already at primary school, so they were often over-anxious to provide parental discipline, and restore the balance of power at home. The homework scenario was outside their experience, as many of them had left school at 14, but they knew that educational achievement was paramount in the real world of work, and they wanted their children to succeed. The pre-war unemployment problems, they remembered all too well, made them uneasy about what might happen in the future.

The pressure to provide homework in English was unremitting. An essay would be set and subsequently handed in. For each pupil, that might represent an hour or so's work, whereas, for the teacher, it meant hours of marking, if the whole exercise were to have any real value. I landed up with piles of exercise books on the floor in the dining room, as every other space had already been taken. When I collected homework from our fifth form, there were always one or two dodgers with excuses that suggested the dog had eaten it, a younger sibling had thrown it on the fire or, perhaps, the book had been left on the bus. Nothing prepared me for the charming smile and apologetic tones that Harry produced, when asked what had happened. "I'm really sorry, but there just wasn't time over the weekend." My reaction was straight off the top of my head. "When you leave school, Harry, you should get a job, smiling at women. You do it very well!" (And I had never, ever said that before to anyone else!).

We had recorded several of the poems on our new reel to reel tape machine, with one of the group strumming his guitar in the background. Auditions, and a vote, had made Harry the undisputed choice to be 'the voice', and the result was quite impressive. There was the odd hiccup, when he read in 'The Snake', "I picked up a CRUMSY log", but otherwise the recording was very professional. Tapes were expensive, so his efforts were soon rubbed out by the next contribution. If only I'd known!

We had Room 9 as a form base, and it quickly became the 5th Form Common Room. They were all prefects, apart from being briefly demoted when they were caught, truanting from school, as they queued for tickets for Bill Hailey at The Regal Edmonton. They had a gramophone, a dartboard, and a kettle to make tea at break time. It was all very civilised. Then came July, and the big test. I was quite pleased with the Language questions, and most of the class seemed to be reasonably happy, when we spoke afterwards. The Literature was a little stiffer but quite within everyone's capability, and the pass mark was only 45%.

We were all rather sad when term ended and the final assembly sang, 'Lord dismiss us with thy blessing' and the wonderful line:

"Let Thy father's hand be shielding, all who here shall meet no more."

It had always given me a lump in my throat, and this time it seemed particularly sad. They enthusiastically hugged each other, and our very first exam class of 16 year olds, left. The big wide world beckoned and they all went off to earn a living. I thought I might never see them again, but it didn't work out like that.

When the exam results came out in mid-August, I was really disappointed. They had nearly all passed English Language with flying colours, but there were several failures in Literature. Janice, as expected, did brilliantly in both. Harry passed Language, but didn't quite make it in Eng Lit.. He got 42%, just three marks short of a pass.

School restarted in September, and it was difficult, at first, to adjust to the new faces in Room 9. The circle of holes in the wall, where the dartboard had been, was a constant reminder of happy days gone by.

My new class of thirteen-year-olds, Middle 3A, were much more of a challenge, as, during the following year they would be able to leave at the end of the particular term in which they reached the statutory school leaving age of fifteen. This did not make for a settled final exit, as the date of birth became a vital part of plans for getting a job. Each term had a set date by which 'to leave or not to leave' was judged. In effect, some of my new form would only have three more terms at school, and many of them were ill-prepared for the world of work. It worried me a lot more than it worried them!

I knew that I would be their form teacher until they left at fifteen, so I determined to run a very tight ship. I worked hard to see that they got as much out of school as they possibly could, and actually enjoyed the experience. I also had them for English five times a week, which was a great help in getting to know them. Our language textbook was Ridout 3, which I liked because of the wide variety of approaches it embodied. To make exercises out of jokes, (rather than the other way round!), was a really good idea, I felt. One went like this:

> 'Two men were eating dinner in a restaurant, and, when the fish course was served, there was a large fish and a small one. The first man took the larger fish. The second man was very put out and commented, angrily, "If I had had the first choice, I would have taken the smaller portion!" "Well, what are you grumbling about?" answered his companion. "You got the smaller one!"'

Even punctuation could be fun.

The poetry anthology that came our way, out of the large English cupboard at the back of the hall, was full of hugely enjoyable poems, some of which were new to me. 'Timothy Winters' by Charles Causley, was a wonderful introduction to a poet I'd barely heard of, and pieces like Edward Lear's 'The Jumblies', gave lots of opportunities for choral speaking, that suited the group, as something for us all to learn by heart. Mary, who was very keen on dancing, (she went on to The Windmill Theatre, after she left school!), did the Tarantella, to our rendering of 'Do you remember an inn, Miranda?', and the class was good at the accompanying rhythmic clapping, thanks to practice on the terraces at White Hart Lane. The number of poems I knew by heart, increased enormously.

The School ran a rather ambitious House System, based on the Public School model The names had been suggested by the history teacher, as having local significance, (nobody seemed to know exactly what), and were called Beaumont, Dacres, Gough and Salisbury. In that order, their special colours were blue, red, green and yellow. Though straight out of college, I had been made House Mistress of Salisbury, the yellow house, with the motto 'Aim High', and I took the unpaid responsibilities very seriously. Lots of 'Holy Family Convent' enthusiasm supporting our teams in various tournaments, football, netball, rugby and rounders, and, of course our athletics team on Sports Day. I loved it and made yellow rosettes and banners, and we cheered till we were hoarse. There was a lot of healthy inter-house rivalry. Janice was a tower of strength in the green house, Gough, and Harry was a sporting star in Dacres, holding the school javelin record for years after he left, and playing soccer in the district team.

On alternate Fridays, there was a house assembly in either the hall, or the dining room, so I tried to build up a team spirit and a loyalty to Salisbury with suitable hymns and prayers. Looking back now, I'm amazed at the things I did, but, at the time, they seemed to work. I even thought of writing a house song, but there wasn't anyone who could write the music, so to my disappointment, and to everyone-else's great relief, I had to abandon the idea.

Meanwhile, back at 'Wits End', things were going well. Ernest had got used to the vagaries of British Rail on his daily journeys to and from Westminster, and, complete with cycle clips, rode off on his bike at 7.30am every morning. Paul was doing splendidly at St Ignatius College at Stamford Hill, and the baby had grown into an energetic toddler, who spent his time with his teddy, Whiney, running in circles, around the apple tree in the middle of the lawn. To Ernest's dismay, the grass gave up the unequal struggle, and a well-used circular running track resulted.

James Douglas was a very endearing little boy, and we all loved hearing the funny things he said. When he left any food at a meal, he would push the plate carefully away, saying "Flo lee birdies!", and if he particularly liked the taste of anything he would ask for, "Some more of some of that.". If he ever felt ill, he would announce, very solemnly, "I aren't well, are I?".

We had also acquired a long-haired black cat called Jinxy and four chickens, each named after a well-endowed film star, Millie, Sophie, Lucy and Lolly, which, when they were on-lay, made certain we were over-supplied with eggs. There are only so many eggs a family can eat, and we gave a lot away. Ernest, assisted by Paul, made sure that the garden was weed free and produced masses of vegetables and flowers, while, at the bottom of the garden, the Spurs training ground kept everyone interested. The boys would sit on the bank and look down on the players working out to the shouted instructions of the coach to "Get your f….. ing legs moving!"

The house was kept spick and span by Mrs Pegram, who came for three hours every weekday morning. She had originally been in service with Lord and Lady someone or other, and had gone with them to the grouse moors, in the shooting season. When she cleaned our brass candlesticks, she told me that his lordship always had a silver pheasant, as a centre-piece on the dining table, so we knew that we weren't quite up to spec, socially.

We had joined Broxbourne Bridge Club and played there once a week, and we owned a red Morris Minor Convertible. Our social life was fine. I had done some amateur drama with Sue, and her new husband, Jim, and we won an award with 'The Happy Journey' at Hertford Drama Festival. If Ernest and I wanted to go out we had a resident baby-sitter in Paul, and we could afford to take family summer holidays at the seaside, in England or Wales. Buddy was now happily retired in Enfield, only about six miles away, so we saw her regularly. She had let part of the house to Curly, who played a lot of social bridge with us. He became a close friend and was a wonderful godfather to little 'Noddy'.

Even with Mrs Pegram's help, I was very busy. There was cooking for the four of us, though Ernest always did the shopping, and the English marking was very time-consuming. There were always piles of exercise books about the house, waiting to be corrected. Nevertheless, in June, when we were invited to a 'Car Rally' by Dorothy, one of the science teachers, we were keen to take part. She lived in Watton-at-Stone, near Stevenage, and it proved to be a very enjoyable evening. We had to drive around a route of about twenty miles, through pretty villages, collecting information along the way. Starting and ending at her house, it was clearly quite competitive, and we took to it like ducks to water. There was a party in the garden afterwards, with delicious refreshments. We didn't win, but we had a great time. What a wonderful idea. I couldn't wait to organise one for my birthday on July 14th.

Of course, ours would be a little bit different; we would have rhymed clues that you had to solve before you knew what you were looking for. Ernest cheerfully accepted the role of route planner, and had an enjoyable time studying ordnance survey maps of the local area, as he sketched out a rough idea of where we would go. We went off after an early supper, and the route was perfect. There would be enough houses and churches to provide material for the clues. I made mental notes of things that might be useful and we found a lovely old country pub that would make a very good halfway house. And so began a great tradition of birthday car rallies that was to continue for the next twenty years or so.

I always had great fun spotting unusual things for clues. There is an endless supply of material, absolutely everywhere. Oddly shaped doors and windows, dates on walls or in churches, and interesting statues in gardens. There are strange demon door knockers, things on windowsills and so on. Look hard enough and you'll find them, and thinking out good clues and rhyming them, was the greatest challenge. We learnt to double check everything or the competitors would be quick to complain, especially if it caused them to miss a clue, or get lost. Winning became very desirable, and woe betide us if we messed things up. But even the best laid plans can go astray.

We found one magnificent oddment in the front garden of a country cottage. It was the chassis of a very old and rusty car, without wheels, and propped up on four piles of bricks. To our delight the number plate was clearly visible, DAD 347. I was quite pleased with my clue, something like,

"Not going places? That's quite clear, but what is father doing here?".

On our final check, the evening before the rally, everything was in place. The route was fine, the clues not too hard and the weather forecast good. The question sheets were all prepared, with Ernest in charge of marking.

All went well until, surprisingly, at the end, Ernest found that everyone had got one answer wrong. No-one had spotted DAD. They all protested that no such old car existed on our route. The next evening, to take a photograph to prove its existence, we drove out to see for ourselves. I'm sure you can guess what happened. The car must have been removed, in the few hours between our final check, the previous evening, and the actual rally. Only the piles of bricks remained to prove it had not been a figment of our imagination!

I loved composing the clues and every year had a favourite. Once there was a notice in someone's garden offering miniature dachshund puppies for sale. It was my best clue that year.

"Cuddly babies, for a starter. Shall we call them chipolata?"

The annual school play had, by now, become a fixture, sometimes at Christmas and sometimes in the Easter Term. It was always difficult to keep up the standard and make each production, the best ever. Perforce, the casts changed all the time, and for the most part were made up of 15 year olds. I used to dread the question, "What are you going to do next?", because I usually hadn't the faintest idea.

We followed 'A Christmas Carol' with a dramatised version of Charles Kingsley's 'The Water Babies', which gave Ken a wonderful chance to show what could be done with exciting scenery, costume and lighting. I shall never forget the underwater scenes, with the jelly fish swirling across the stage. It was all done with umbrellas and trailing fronds, but they looked magnificent, in front of a cyclorama painted with a huge wrecked galleon. The story is a Victorian moral fable, about Tom, the poor little chimney sweep and the ubiquitous Mrs Do-as-you-would-be-done-by, (very well played by Monica, who had been a rabbit in 'Toad of Toad Hall'), and to my surprise, everyone seemed to enjoy it. "What are you going to do next?" they said. I gave my answer at a staff party several years later, singing it to the tune of a song I had learnt when I was a Girl Guide, 'Too-rooli-aye'.

WHAT'S NEXT?

As a teacher of drama in school you may find,
There is something that constantly preys on your mind
For there's one special question you just dread to hear
And it's, "Well, and which play are you doing next year?"

Chorus: Singing, too-roo-li, too-roo-li, too-roo-li-ay

For the play that you choose may have many defects
But I fear that it just mustn't be about sex,
No double entendres, not risqué or lewd,
No 'To hell with the costumes let's work in the nude!

It'll be controversial if it's about God,
Or politics, or violence, or just a bit odd,
And don't put on The Hostage, that would be absurd.
What on earth would you do with that four letter word?

You could try Molière in original French
And then no-one will know what is said to the wench,
Or Goethe in German...... Euripides in Greek......
Or those old plays in Russian, that last for a week.

If your Drama Adviser is devil-may-care,
He'll support to the hilt your production of 'Hair',
Though it seems far more likely, 'cos you can't please 'em all,'
That you'll end up, once more, doing 'Toad of Toad Hall'!

Chapter 6

The fifties had run their course, and we all looked forward to the new decade. Keith and I were firm friends and we used to play tennis together after school on Wednesdays. He got on very well with Ernest and was great at DIY, which was very useful. Janice had decided that an office job with ICI was not for her, and to my great delight, had come to 'Wits End', to ask my advice about training to be a teacher. Naturally, I offered to introduce her to the Principal of Trent Park, H.A.T.Simmons. I knew he would welcome her with open arms, and I rang him to ask if they could ignore the fact that she did not have the requisite 'A levels'. I told him that she would be a perfect student, and would make a wonderful teacher. We went, together, to see him, and she started there the following term.

There was pressure on me to do a play that would give some of the staff a chance to act, so I looked for something in the fairy tale line, for the following Christmas. I spent one Saturday at French's in London and came up with just the thing in 'The Heartless Princess'. It had lots of parts for the children, and three great chances for adults to show their paces, as the King, a mad Duchess and her mortal enemy, the Fox. There were plenty of small parts in the members of the court, plus a beautiful Princess and her ladies-in-waiting, a handsome young Prince and his entourage. Just what we wanted.

The head of English, Mick, a very good actor, was keen to play the dithering, ineffectual King, and Keith wanted to be the scheming Fox, who fights a never-ending battle of wits with the Duchess. We had Princesses and Princes galore, plus courtiers and nurses and so on. At first I was only going to direct, but there just wasn't anyone to play the mad Duchess so, with a suitable show of reluctance, I grabbed the opportunity! I hadn't realised quite how demanding the dual role would be, and I kept having to readjust the whole stage picture, to include me. My New York friends, Bob and Mary, who were doing medical research in London, brought their children, Carol and Paul, to see the play, and they came backstage afterwards. Thanks to a wonderfully scary purple make-up by Ken, the children didn't recognise me, and hid behind their parents, lest the mad Duchess should put a spell on them, as she had on the poor princess.

Keith and I had a wonderful time playing against each other. The Fox had to hide in a big wicker hamper, opening and closing the lid at exactly the right moment, so that the Duchess couldn't see him. We got it down to a fine art, so that the audience gasped with relief as the lid came down with only seconds to spare, and the Fox was safe!

The advent of the sixties was full of hope. The School had settled down well and class sizes had gone down from over 40 to a mere 35, so that I didn't have to seat people on the window sill any more, because there weren't enough chairs. The staff was stable, very few people leaving and all of us getting more confident in the success of the secondary modern experiment. We were non-selective, which meant we had some children from the local gypsy encampment, who, occasionally, went off to fairgrounds in the summer, plus quite well-off middle class pupils from big houses in Cuffley. Yet it all worked. The school plays were the best in the area, our games teams were very successful, nearly everyone wore school uniform and we even had a fifth form taking O level. As we did not offer A level studies, most of the pupils didn't even think of trying to get into university. For those who did, a transfer to Cheshunt Grammar School could be arranged, and they would go on from there.

We had started a Commercial Course for girls who wanted to stay on after fifteen, and in Room 9 the clatter of typewriter keys could be heard, coming from Room 12, at the top of the staircase. A middle-aged businessman turned teacher, Charley, ran his own little empire, giving training in shorthand, typing, book-keeping and general office procedure. It was his world and he allowed no interference. He was also a bridge player, and we had started a foursome at lunch time. He loved a good argument, though it was impossible ever to pin him down, as he was the master of outrageous non-sequiturs. I wrote the following, especially for him:

FOR CHARLEY

It's not hard disagreeing with Charley,
For you know all along that you're right,
Quarrels vary, from merely a parley
To a stand-up, outspoken, big fight.
When it happens at Bridge it's quite funny,
If you say he put you in a fix
With one jack in his hand, and he's dummy,
And he raised your 'one club' up to six.
Then he's likely to quickly remember
That occasion you shirked a finesse,
Or, how twelve months ago last December,
You lost that important address.
While you're struggling to find the connection,
He has asked you to clearly explain
Why you didn't support the election
Of someone he'd rather not name.
Now that leads him to question your reason
For moving your house in the snow,
When, throughout last year's badminton season,
He had noticed you just didn't go.
Well, by now, you're so utterly muddled
That you don't know the short from the long,
So you say, I'm completely befuddled,
But once more, my dear Charles, YOU ARE WRONG!

A big new bonus for the whole area was the emergence of our very own pop star in 'Cliff Richard'. He had already had wonderful success in the charts with 'Move It', and was obviously going to go a long way. I was especially delighted to have been proved wrong, as I had liked him very much at school, and had strongly advised him not to give up his day job in an office to go into pop music! Ah well!

He gave very generously of his time, raising funds for local Boys' Clubs and for our School. We often met when I was responsible for staging the events, either at school or at The Regal, Edmonton, and with Cliff, we always played to packed houses. He willingly signed autographs and I was amused to see that he would write 'Sincerely', as I had once made him correct a misspelling of the word, a hundred times, saying, "You never know how important, in the future, this word could be for you". I was, clearly, a clair voyante!

I followed 'The Heartless Princess' with another fairy tale, 'The Emperor's Nightingale', this time for pupils only. It went down well with the audience, but I hadn't ever really liked the story, and thought it was not up to our usual standard, so when Keith offered to write a script for a future play I jumped at the idea. We had spoken before about the story of 'Pinocchio', and I had even borrowed a dramatised version from French's, but it was stilted and rather dreary. Such a good story demanded a much better script, and Keith wanted to make one from the original story. When he did it I was overjoyed. It was perfect!

At the time, we had exactly the right people in school. A tall, chubby 16 year old Greek-Cypriot boy, called Aggie, to play Gepetto, and a very able thirteen year old, Philip, for the lead role. Our Pinocchio was slightly uncoordinated in his movements, and took to being a puppet with consummate ease. There was a large cast, all very good in rehearsal, except the Cat, who with the Fox, leads Pinocchio astray. She just couldn't remember her lines with any degree of accuracy.

When Keith came into rehearsals, it really annoyed him. She would make up stumbling, ungrammatical dialogue, that bore little or no resemblance to his extremely witty lines. He wanted me to get rid of her, but I hadn't the heart, as she was a very keen member of the group and was really trying hard to do better. In the end we compromised. She kept the part, we gave all her good lines to the Fox, but she didn't mind a bit!

Yet again, our school play was a great success. Cliff came to one of the performances, but I kept him backstage, so that the audience wouldn't see him and get over-excited. He did the make-up for some of the cast, including Stephen, playing the fisherman, who was really thrilled to get such VIP treatment, and who still remembers it, over fifty years later. Gepetto was a difficult part for a boy, but Aggie gave such a mature performance that, the following year, I cast him as the lead in André Obey's 'Noah', and he was brilliant.

The Staff had been virtually unchanged for some time, apart from the arrival of David, a lively new Head of French. He was in his mid-twenties, but when he came on interview, I had met him, walking on the wrong side of the main corridor. I thought he was one of the older boys, and started to tell him off, and it wasn't until I noticed that he had a moustache, that I realised my mistake. Shortly afterwards, the Head of RE retired, and we were delighted to welcome a young replacement called Bill. He fitted in wonderfully well, keeping his head down and making a really good impression on both staff and pupils. Religious Education has never been an easy subject to teach. Faith is such a personal thing, and so difficult to pass on to others, without seeming to try to 'convert' them to your own beliefs. Somehow, Bill was able to manage this difficult juggling act, without seeming either smug or wishy-washy. He had originally been a journalist, and he had run 'Crusader' groups for boys at his local church. He had become an excellent teacher, so discipline wasn't a problem.

Just before he arrived, I had asked the headmaster, if Keith and I could take a party on one of the new School Cruises aboard, the P & O ship, 'Nevasa'. It would be for fourteen days, in the Easter Term, and involved travelling to Genoa by train, and boarding the ship there for a cruise around the Mediterranean. We were to visit Venice, Malta, Athens and Sicily, and would only cost the pupils just over £40 each. If we took a party of 35, we could take three members of staff, free! The Head agreed to let us tell the school and see what happened.

Within a week, we had taken deposits for all thirty-five places, and even had a waiting list, in case anyone dropped out. The next thing to settle was, who should come with us? There were several teachers neither of us wanted to go anywhere with for a day, let alone for fourteen, so we couldn't ask for volunteers. I suggested to Keith that the new chap, Bill, looked really nice, and though he seemed very quiet, I was sure we would both get on well with him. Bill said that he would like to come, and it worked out beautifully.

He was very good company, and, on the journey to Genoa, across Europe by train, he was a tower of strength. We had sleeping compartments, boys and girls separately, but, of course, that segregation was very soon ended, when the girls invaded the boys' carriage. I was overtired, and furious when I caught them, but Bill managed to inject a cheerful common sense into the 'disaster', and order was quickly restored. I noticed that he had lovely blue eyes and a great sense of humour.

When we got to the ship it was wonderful. The students were all in single sex dormitories and there was a tight patrol by the ship's staff to make sure that there were no breaches of the arrangements. They had a built in 'punishment' for any funny business, that involved making the culprits get fully dressed, and run round the deck till they were tired out. Word had spread that this wasn't any fun, and so absolutely no-one broke the rules. All their meals were in a supervised dining space, with menus chosen to be enjoyed by unadventurous teenagers, including dishes like sausage and mash.

Happily, it was not like that for us. Though we had to share cabins with people we didn't know, everything else was geared to making the cruise an enjoyable experience for the teachers. We had the same mealtime arrangements as the paying customers, which meant wonderfully varied and exciting menus, including the luxury of things like lobster. There was lots to do, after the pupils' bedtime, and cigarettes and alcohol were tax free. We had a great cruise. We taught the lessons, and did the supervision duties, we were expected to do. Keith, as the maths expert, organised pocket money, in the right currency, to take ashore or spend on board. We danced with the group in the evening and ferried them around foreign ports, when the ship docked. I have a picture of the three of us, in St Mark's Square, in Venice, and we are, clearly, having a very good time.

When we got back to school, it was obvious that we had been sorely missed. Staff had lost free periods taking our classes, and had not been happy about our two week absence. However, we promised that, in future, we would go in the holidays, so 'The School Cruise ' became a fixture for the next few years. We were never short of applicants, as word soon spread that it was great fun.

Once the school holidays were involved, Keith opted out, but Bill, and his Crusader chum, Graham, came, and we all danced the 'Twist', and, stamp, stamped, 'Glad All Over'. On one cruise, Cliff came out and joined us in Madeira, for a day or two. To everyone's delight, he gave a concert on the open deck to all the passengers, spending time training some of the guitar playing pupils, to act as a backing group. He did it wonderfully well, and Cheshunt Secondary Modern's reputation got a great boost. The next voyage was to the Baltic, and my travelling companion was Charley, the teacher in charge of our school's Commercial Course, but that's another story!

Finally, Paul agreed to come. He had spent a year in an international school in Lausanne, as an unqualified teacher of English, and had the great advantage of being able to play the guitar. When the weather got rough, and most of the party felt seasick, we kept them up on deck, singing naughty songs like, 'Oh, he's got a lovely naval uniform', to give them something else to think about. He worked hard, and was very good company, even making up a jingle, to teach the group a few Spanish phrases, to use in Majorca. To this day, we still occasionally let rip with:

"Aye, aye, aye-aye, donde esta el barco ? Habla usted ingles, por favor? Si? No? Muchas gracias!"

After that, the cost of the cruises greatly increased, and so we stopped going.

James Douglas, still affectionately called 'Noddy', had started school in 1961. As I had a full-time teaching job, before that, he had been looked after during the day, by a combination of mother's helps and nursery schools. He was a delightful little boy, intelligent, loving and out-going, and everyone liked him. He was already very good at sport, and his running track on the lawn was in constant use. After a brief spell at the Convent in Hoddesdon, we sent him to 'Brooklands', a local primary school, run by a neighbour in Pine Close.

Stafford was from Northern Ireland, with an accent you could cut with a knife, and 'Brooklands' was successful, very conventional and geared to getting good results, in a happy atmosphere. The pupils wore blazers, striped in light blue and navy, which looked very much like those of an expensive prep school. They had a male deputy head, who taught football and cricket to the boys, and altogether the pupils were given a very good start to their school careers.

At home, Noddy let us hear the hymns that he had learnt for school assembly. In 'Fight the good fight', Christians were instructed, not to lay hold on life, but quite categorically to 'Lay hold a knife'. In his version of 'To be a pilgrim', we learnt that, "He, who would valiant be, GAINS all disaster". How very true! I relayed all the revised lines to Keith, and, catching each other's eye, we would secretly sing them, at our school assemblies, whenever the chance came.

Not surprisingly, I couldn't resist the temptation of parodying the verse of a hymn, at the end of the staff party entertainment. Bill, Keith and I sang:

"Now thank the L E A,
the term has almost ended,
There's only one more day
in which to get suspended.
But there's one other thing
we have to ask of Thee.
Though school should end at four
Please may we go at three?"

Chapter 7

In Enfield, time was beginning to take its toll on Buddy. Now in her eighties, she had been given a sleeping pill called 'Thalidomide', and the result was disastrous. She developed peripheral neuritis, which gave her permanent 'pins and needles' in her hands and feet. It broke her. From a positive, active, if older, retired professional woman, still cycling everywhere, she became a nervous wreck. We tried having her to live with us at 'Wits End', but she needed someone to be with her all the time, so we found a comfortable old people's home, where she would have lots of company, in nearby Hoddesdon.

The Matron in charge of 'Belmont House' was not a state registered nurse so, quite naturally, Buddy offered advice on any medical problem that arose. The other inmates were always the 'old people', though many of them were much younger than she was. She settled down surprisingly well, coming to Cheshunt on Sundays for lunch, and she seemed reasonably happy. Inevitably, she finally went downhill and ended up in hospital in Bishops Stortford. Peggy and I visited her and, though she was in pain, she wanted to know how we were. I said, "It's dull in our town since my playmates left...". She recognised the line at once, and, for the last time, without hesitation, finished the tale of 'The Pied Piper'. She fell into a coma two days later, and died on December 5th, 1966, the day of the Staff Party.

Not long after, on a 'Creative Writing Course' for English teachers, we were set the task of writing a poem. I had loved and admired Buddy, and she called me her 'little pal', which was the greatest compliment I could have had. Although she had been short of money, as even matrons were not well paid, I had been privately educated, and she always supported my 'good ideas', never grumbling if they proved to be expensive failures.

THE DISTRICT NURSE

Purposeful and practical, she buzzed
Her way through other people's lives,
In ceaseless doing good. Not saving souls
For some eternal bliss, but saving time
And getting something done

Insistent rapping on the door
Warned relative and victim, "Nurse is here",
And, when she left, the patient lay
In unaccustomed neatness,
Comforted and treated.

To queue for shopping nearly drove her mad
So, marching to the counter, she would say,
"I am a nurse, and so I cannot wait!"
And she'd be served, and, briskly hurry off,
And no-one seemed to mind.

And when, at last, she simply wore away,
Her funeral hearse crawled slowly to the place
Where she must rest at last. But, even there,
Another cortege stood, while other mourners
Wept for other dead.

And then the simple coffin seemed to shake
As if to push away the sealing wreaths,
And bone chafed bone, resentful at delay.
"Now, hurry, for you see I am a nurse,
And, therefore, I cannot wait!"

It was actually true. The Enfield crematorium had been busy, and funerals were running late. When our cortege arrived, it had to wait in a queue, until the previous funerals were over.

At times, school could be rather trying, despite the good company of friends like Keith and Bill, and the usual jolly japes at Christmas, or on birthday car rallies. Cliff's career was going brilliantly and we went to concerts and TV shows where he always seemed to be surrounded by screaming fans. Despite all his success he was as likeable, and as unspoiled as ever, and we did an entertainment for one of the staff parties together. I parodied some of his songs like

'Young ones, we used to be the young ones.....'

and 'Lucky Lips' that became:

'Spreading Hips are never welcome, but they seem to grow on you,
Suddenly from thirty-six you've jumped to forty-two....'

We had great fun rehearsing at the house in Totteridge. Both he and Janice had become close friends, and Jan's talented artist husband, Mike, had been one of my special favourites from the very first time I had met him.

School plays were still making good headlines in the local press, and we seemed to have success after success. A production of 'Tobias and the Angel' had nearly hit disaster. By sheer chance, walking down the corridor outside the secretary's office I had spotted my star player, 'The Angel', apparently waiting to see the Headmaster. "Are you in trouble?" I asked. His answer shook me to the core, "No, miss, but I'm leaving next week, so I have to take a form home for my dad to sign."

We had been rehearsing the play for six weeks and I had just another month to polish up the production. "You can't be leaving," I stuttered. "What about the play?" It seemed that he had been going to tell me that very evening, at rehearsal, that he wouldn't be able to be in it. They were moving to Dorset the following week. I was, for once, speechless.

What I could do to save the play, was not immediately obvious. In a school production there are no understudies for the main parts. If you are good enough to be an understudy, you already have an important role in your own right. It was a male part, so I couldn't play it myself. Who could be my 'Angel'?

Then the obvious answer hit me, Keith! He was a very good actor and had had parts in several plays done by the local amateur dramatic society. He had been wonderful as the Fox in 'The Heartless Princess', and he would be totally reliable. He wouldn't get ill or decide to leave Cheshunt next week. To cut a long story short, when I asked him, he was delighted. He had read the play and had thought that the Angel was a superb part. The answer was definitely, yes. He proved to be as good as I had hoped he would be, and even grew a goatee beard, which suited the role to perfection. He knew the very long part within a week, and never needed a prompt. We all totally forgot that he had not been our Angel from the start. I breathed a sigh of relief.

But Fate had not yet finished with 'Tobias and the Angel'. Three days before the dress rehearsal, the girl who was to play Anna, Tobias's wife, was taken ill with glandular fever. She was desperately disappointed, but there was absolutely no chance that she would recover in time. She was about my size, so her costume would fit me, and I knew the part from nearly three months of rehearsal. So I played it !

Harold Wilson's Labour government in Westminster was, at the time, making changes that would affect our lives in rural Hertfordshire. The apparent inequality of opportunity, produced by the Butler Act and the 11+ selection tests, was to be put right. The Grammar Schools were seen as Tory heartlands, creating and exacerbating class differences. It looked a real vote catcher, and it was the death knell of the Secondary Modern experiment. The new buzz word was 'Comprehensive'. Change the name, and any problems would miraculously disappear under the new dispensation. The fact that Harold Wilson, himself, owed his success to the educational opportunities given to working class boys and girls by the grammar schools, went unnoticed. Change was on the way.

It hit us, in Cheshunt, almost overnight. With the same pupils and the same staff, we suddenly got a new identity, RIVERSMEAD. Our school blazer badge and tie had a pattern, designed by the Art Department, of two wavy white lines on a navy background, which represented the two rivers in the area. The larger one, the Lea, rose in Luton, and joined the Thames near Wapping. The other was the New River, which was not really a river at all, but a canal, constructed in early Victorian times to ensure a drinking-water supply for London, from natural springs at Great Amwell. The new name raised a few eyebrows, someone remarking that it sounded like a rest home for horses, but, like it or not, we were now 'Riversmead Comprehensive School', and John Newsom, the Chief Education Officer of Hertfordshire, was the new messiah.

Quite naturally, with all these changes in the air, I wrote something for the Staff Party that Bill, Keith and I, dressed as teenagers, delivered.

A SCHOOL SONG FOR THE MIDDLE FOURTHS

We're the Newsom Fourth Formers of Riversmead,
And the wavy line badge is our mark,
We love summer's sun, but the winter's more fun
Because we go home in the dark!

The County must find us expensive
For we lose every pencil and book,
But, surely, you see, as we get them all free,
We're not quite as dim as we look!

In order to get the insurance,
We've set several classrooms on fire,
And all of us girls have a yen to wear pearls, (Mr Pearl
was the music master!)
So we're thinking of joining the choir.

We'll soon have to work for a living
And when we are husbands and wives,
We'll think times at school, when we all played the fool,
Were the cushiest days of our lives.

Our old headmaster was now nearing retirement, and had become, it seemed to me, progressively less flexible. He was suspicious of the many changes brought about by the 'Comprehensive' initiatives, and certainly did not want misguided enthusiasts on the staff, considering new ways of doing things. I was pretty sure that he thought of me as 'a loose cannon', and, though, I think, he appreciated the accolades that the plays brought for the school, he always took the compliments personally, with a wry, surprised smile. I really liked Riversmead, and did not want to leave, but, after Buddy's death, it seemed a good time to try to get away for a bit. I had heard about taking 'a year on secondment', on full salary, but it sounded too good to be true. I could study something in depth, but what?

I came up, finally, with 'English as a Foreign Language'. I didn't know much about it, but it sounded interesting. I spoke to the Head about releasing me, on secondment for a year, and I had never seen him so enthusiastic. He positively glowed, and didn't even ask which particular branch of education I planned to enliven with my presence. Of course he would support ANY application I might make. He loved the idea.

Only then did I start investigating the actual EFL courses. A requirement, at the end of the year, it seemed, was a month's residence in a foreign country. I could see myself basking in the Mediterranean sunshine, having conversations in Spanish, or Italian, or French, with charming, intelligent adults. Alas, when I got the full details, the high spot was a month's stay in rural Wales. They promised the added attraction of an introduction to, 'The problems of Welsh speakers in a Modern Society'. I already knew about those. We had a large contingent of teachers from Wales on our staff, and when they wanted to be particularly annoying, they would chat to each other in Welsh. They even called themselves 'The Tafia'.

EFL was a definite non-starter and the time for applications for secondment was running out. The Head anxiously reminded me of his full support, and the urgency of the matter. Then I thought of Drama. I had done English, with Drama, at Trent Park, and I actually included improvisation in occasional lessons, especially on a Friday afternoon.

I ran the School Dramatic Society as an extra-curricular activity, and everybody said we did very good productions. I could hardly need a whole year to work on skills I felt I already had, but it was now or never, if 1967 was to be my year of release.

I scoured 'The Times Ed' for information, and discovered that 'The Central School of Speech and Drama', in London, had just what I was looking for. It was called an ' Advanced Course in Speech and Drama for Qualified Teachers', and when I told the Head, he was clearly very pleased. If I needed time to go for a visit, just let him know. There would be no problem. I made a rather hurried application to Central and to my delight, (and the Head's), I was called for an interview.

That day, in the spring of 1967, is, forever, branded on my memory. At the start, all went well. There were seven other applicants for the course, three men and four women, and we all looked suitably harassed. A series of tests took us, separately, to different locations, in the rather gloomy premises at Swiss Cottage. I was able to repeat a tapped-out rhythm, tell if one note was higher or lower than another, and hum a simple tune. I felt increasingly confident. Then came the improvisation that should clinch my acceptance.

One extremely charming man on the interviewing panel, leant forward. "Imagine you are at home and you realise that the house is on fire. You have a child asleep in an upstairs room and you must go and wake him. You know that he has a terrible fear of fire and is liable to panic, yet if he is to escape from the house it is necessary for him to remain calm. Right? Think about it, then start as soon as you're ready."

My mind went totally blank. I knew real panic, as in that nightmare when you're crossing a road, and your legs give way. I stumbled into the space that awaited my performance. Desperately, I focused on an area of the floor, and spoke to it, urgently. "Wake up, sweetheart, the house is on fire!" I moved my eyes upwards, to a spot on the wall. "Don't worry, darling, here comes the fireman!" I gave the panel a nervous, apologetic smile. There was a moment's silence, then they realised that nothing more was going to happen, and that was that.

The interview that followed went by in a blur of shame. To the question on why I felt I needed to do a course in drama, I managed to say that, maybe, my failure in the improvisation was the obvious answer. They nodded in agreement. I was pretty sure that they wouldn't be choosing me for an advanced study of anything. However, very much to my surprise, they decided to accept me on the course, and I started my amazing year at Central in September, 1967.

Paul was training to be a teacher at Balls Park College, in Hertford, having found the psychology degree course at London University, distinctly not to his taste. James, now 11, had been offered a place at either Cheshunt Grammar School or a new grammar school, just around the corner, at Goffs Oak and, on Stafford's recommendation, we opted for Cheshunt. I was puzzled that, just as the secondary moderns were being made comprehensive, the county was actually opening a new grammar school so close by.

To my chagrin, Riversmead appeared to be going to be able to get on perfectly well without me, though of course, there would be no school play. I would be seeing Keith at weekends to keep up with the gossip, and he was fascinated by the prospect of finding out what really happened in drama schools. Ernest was, as ever, a tower of strength and completely understood why I needed a temporary change of direction. He invariably showed a great interest in all my new adventures, so long as his own daily routine was not in danger of being disturbed. Mrs Pegram would do the household chores, so there should be no problems at 'Wits End', and I made a huge effort and got all my English marking done, so that our dining room floor was once again visible. I said my goodbyes at school, and I was all set for my year on secondment.

Chapter 8

Driving into London from Cheshunt every day, proved to be a fairly harrowing experience. It was impossible to avoid the first five miles on the main A 10, at rush hour, but once I reached the borders of Enfield, I learnt to weave my way through terraced side streets to Swiss Cottage. It usually took about an hour, but any unforeseen traffic jams could sometimes double that. Getting back in the evening was slightly easier, as we were often expected to stay until six, or later, by which time the congestion on the roads had usually cleared. Nearly all the seven others on the course, were from faraway places, like the north of England, so they either lived in student digs or with friends. They could all easily get to Swiss Cottage, and were glad not to have to bring their cars to central London, where parking spaces were horrendously difficult to come by.

They seemed to have a wide variety of interests and experience, and, as usual, I liked some much better than others, but there were only eight of us, so I tried to get on with everyone. When all was said and done, we were stuck with each other, at very close quarters, for a whole year. My particular chums were to be Michael, who was very clever and had been teaching in a training college in North Wales, and John, a lovable young Catholic priest from Ireland. After the course, he was going to teach communication skills, to even younger priests-to-be, in the seminary in Dublin.

Jill was, also, great fun. She had a lovely dry sense of humour and taught English in a London grammar school. Two of the others were Chris, a very pretty Canadian girl, and Julian, who proved to have two left feet in the dancing sessions, and is still the only person I have ever met who could really wiggle his ears. Beryl, from Liverpool, and Tony from London, completed the CSD group.

We were very lucky, in that our tutor was a man of outstanding ability. Now in his early forties, Philip had been trained at Central, in the days when The Albert Hall had been its HQ. He had a wonderful enthusiasm for his subject that I found very appealing. At our first educational drama session, he made his entry, by doing an extravagant cartwheel down the centre of a cold and draughty church hall. All the money fell out of his pockets, and I immediately liked him. Within a very short time, we had all settled down in a strange new world of phonetics, speech training, movement and dance, play writing, rehearsals, and all the razzamatazz of drama school life.

I loved the poetry sessions with Philip, and quickly discovered that there was one writer I had somehow missed out on. T S Eliot had not been a part of my convent experience with Sankey, and, though I had loved his cat poems in various anthologies, I had found his plays slightly heavy going. Nothing had prepared me for the impact of 'The Love Song of J. Alfred Prufrock', and I enjoyed the poem so much that I learnt it by heart. Ernest quickly became a T. S. Eliot admirer, as he checked my efforts to remember the lines accurately.

Initially, each of the group had been given a poem to prepare, as a test of vocal skills. Naturally, I committed mine to memory, what else? To my surprise, no-one else did, and they were equally amazed that I had actually learnt the lines. They certainly had not been convent school educated by Sankey!

After lunch in the canteen, Michael and I used to wander around Swiss Cottage, laughing as we tried out the latest strange sound combinations we had met in phonetics. He knew some spectacular ways of remembering lists of unrelated objects, and was an expert in lateral thinking. He was, also, very good at inventing dialogue, a skill that I totally lacked. Play writing sessions were a nightmare for me, so, one week, I made my offering in verse.

THE SAD TALE OF WOODEN-HEADED JAY

The tale of wooden-headed Jay, who simply couldn't write a play,
Is one, I fear, that sad to tell, a group at Central knew full well.
Each Monday, Charles, the best of men, would ask all CSD's to pen
A little playlet, just to prove dramatic purpose in a move
Or joke, or game. Or else to do "A crisis dialogue for two."

Poor Jay would go back home that night, and think, and think, till morning's light
Began to break in eastern skies, yet not a play could she devise.
She'd sit and scratch her silly head, and wrack her brains, but nothing led
To dialogue that sounded graphic, or plot with overtones dramatic.
She tried, (oh, what a wicked sin,), to oil her wooden head with gin,
With brandy, whisky, even wine, but still she couldn't write a line.
The paper blank, the biro still, not one word done, try as she will.
So, finally, with gesture rash, she'd write a lot of silly trash
Then hang her head, so full of shame, for seven days, till Monday came.

And once more, in The Davis Block, she'd brace herself to take the shock
Of hearing others in the group read out their latest brilliant scoop.
(Perhaps unluckily for Jay, they all knew how to write a play!)
Bright Beryl had a lot of nous, and wrote in shining spurts of Scouse,
While clever Mike, with words so few, could situations well construe.

Young Julian's agile brain employed some strange adventures, straight from Freud,
Then John would, with his winning smile, tell incidents from Erin's Isle.
Both gentle Jill and charming Chris, wrote scenes, that seemed to Jay, just bliss,
And kindly Tony found his place in daring deeds from Outer Space.

So Jay would try to be the last, and read hers over very fast.
The only things that she could write were just suburban, dull and trite.
In fact, it would be true to say, she simply couldn't write a play.
Perhaps, when many years have passed, her kindly tutor may be asked
If he can call to mind, the fools that he has taught in Drama Schools?
Then, maybe, with a little frown, he'll up and take his Memoirs down,
And there, he'll find. (In Volume Two), a note of what he'd tried to do
With all his talent and resource, on Central School's play-writing course.
And then he'll sigh, "Well, there was Jay. She never learnt to write a play!"

The group were amused, but it didn't get me off the hook. All the tutor said was, "Ah, pastiche? Not quite what was needed…".

There was, finally, to be an exam test of our play-writing skills, and I was anxious about the outcome. I needn't have worried. Michael and John carried me through it. I thought up a plot and they simply improvised the dialogue as they went along. All I had to do, was write down what they said. The result, "And the devil's not so bad, either", was a delightfully funny scene, about a very superstitious Irishman, who, accidentally, calls up a leprechaun from the spirit world. John was hilarious as the Irishman, exaggerating his already strong brogue, and we came up with the splendid idea of the 'little fellar' spirit, making its first appearance as a puppet. Michael, in a leprechaun costume to match the puppet, then emerged, full size, from behind a screen. It was all great fun and I was very grateful.

I acted in Michael's play, which was absolutely brilliant. He wrote it especially for me, and I loved doing it. It was a monologue, the story of a very disturbed landlady who had an imaginary affair with one of her tenants. You heard the man's footsteps, you never saw him. She was definitely mad, and though the part was very demanding, I really enjoyed playing it, and the script was so good, it was a rip roaring success.

I found phonetics fascinating and our tutor, Philip, invented wonderful words like YANKSIPASHENDORF, to keep us on our aural toes. The actual acting and production techniques were, I felt, less well covered. The idea that every actor can challenge the moves given by the director, seemed to me to be a recipe for chaos. I had directed quite a few school plays, and shuddered at the thought of having to justify my overall stage pictures to adolescent questioners. I was amused at an incident when Jill, the nicest and least aggressive member of the group, was directing Chris. The Canadian girl was quite sparky and liked the thought of putting any new ideas to the test, so she had queried a move that Jill, as director, had given her. "Why do I go over there?" she asked. Jill was getting tired and the answer was uncharacteristically brusque, "Because I say so!" It was just as I thought: it simply wouldn't work.

Central is, primarily, a school for the training of actors, and learning to direct is a very important part of the course. We were told that the eight of us were to be 'casts', in pairs, for the various productions put on, by the acting students, for their final exam. It sounded interesting, and when I heard that I was paired with John, the young Irish priest, I was absolutely delighted. We both enjoyed comedy and I was sure we could do rather well in the right play, and secure for our director, whoever he was, a pretty good final grade. The possibility of being lumbered with a totally unsuitable play, had never even crossed my mind.

Our director, Griff, was about twenty-two, arrogant and singularly lacking in sensitivity. There was no discussion: he handed us each a copy of something called, 'An Eagle Has Two Heads', and told us which parts we would be playing. We should read the play and rehearsals would start the following week. I said that I hoped I had been chosen for a comic role, as I felt this would let me help him to do well in the exam. Griff frowned, turned away grunting, "See you on Monday", and left.

When John and I read the play, we were both horrified. It was the story of the Empress Elizabeth of Austria, so beautiful that men fainted at the sight of her, who gets murdered by a sexually crazed assassin. I was to be the Empress. I had left my twenties behind, several years previously, and dear Ernest was the only person in the world to think I could even compete in the Miss Universe competition. John was in his twenties, but a priest, dedicated to a life of chastity and self-denial. There was absolutely no humour in the text. It was all blood and thunder.

My immediate reaction was to refuse to do it, then, (remembering that I, also, was being assessed for a final grade), to try to talk Griff into choosing a different play. It was difficult for us. In this particular situation we were just actors, and had to do as we were told, so, when all else had failed, I played the 'age' card. I said, (and it hurt), that I was too old. Griff replied that Sarah Bernhardt had played Juliet when she was over seventy. I said, good for her, but I wasn't Sarah Bernhardt. He suggested that I might be surprised at the heights I could achieve, if I really tried. He had absolutely no intention of changing the play and rehearsals would start the following Monday.

John was much calmer about the whole thing, and so I decided not to make any further fuss. At least I would get killed by the nicest sex-crazed assassin in the whole world. I also realised that, in the exam, not even the utmost 'suspension of disbelief ' would make the final performance acceptable to an audience, so Griff was probably shooting himself in the foot. We were stuck with this farce and all we could do was enjoy it

The first real problem came with the kiss, and, as the would-be assassin and the Empress clearly knew each other quite well, the embrace was supposed to be passionate, and had to look real. John and I tried the close hug, cheek to cheek, nose to nose, that on a stage, seen from the front, can look like a proper kiss. Unfortunately, we were to play 'in the round', so no such subterfuge would work. We had to go lips to lips. We needed some private rehearsals, and that was when I started to feel guilty.

It was a pleasure to kiss John, and to my horror, I found practice sessions enjoyable. It was dreadful. He was a young priest, newly ordained and I felt I was sullying an innocent. Naturally I didn't share these thoughts with him, but my nervous reaction to the situation, made me start to giggle, as the moment for action drew near. The more Griff ground his teeth in fury, the worse I got. I really did try to stop, but I just couldn't, and silent, suppressed laughter would grip me, a page before the actual kiss. It wasn't long before John caught the infection, and we would stand, lip to lip, shaking helplessly with giggles.

At the first read-through, it was obvious that the play was full of lines that, once the heroine was not Sarah Bernhardt, sounded totally inappropriate. When a young aide-de-camp stared at me, I had to say, "What are you looking at?" His reply was, "I'm looking at Beauty!" I gasped. "He certainly can't say that! It'll bring the house down! "He thought for a second and then said, quite seriously, "Well, I could always look out of the window!"

When the dress rehearsal came, Griff dropped another bombshell. He wanted my hair to be drawn back tightly, from a centre parting, in the least flattering style possible. The long practice skirt was to be bunched at the back, to form a pseudo-bustle, which added about six inches to my hip measurement. I wasn't even going to be able to look my normal best. I was on a hiding to nothing.

The final performance in the Embassy Theatre, packed with tutors and students, was unforgettable. For the first time we were all in full costume and the aide-de-camp was wearing real spurs on his boots. As he strode across the stage, the little wheels on the spurs, spun round with a loud whirring sound, that caught everyone's attention. Then came our kiss, after which John was supposed to stab me in the back, as he tightly embraced me. I had to gasp, pull away from him and reach a hand around my back, to the supposed 'wound'.

The dramatic moment was to be when I brought my hand back to look at it, and saw that it was covered in blood. I had to have the blood capsule in my hand throughout the scene, before breaking it open at the right moment, immediately after the kiss. Nervous tension didn't help, but this was the very first time I had tried to perforate its plastic shell. This was very tough and though I dug at it fiercely with my nails, it stayed intact. I let out groans, gasps, sighs and every other sound of pain I could think of, all the time secretly clawing with my nails at the shell of the capsule. Finally, I felt the sticky dampness of the 'blood', so I clutched my back, showed my red stained hand to the world and, to everyone's relief, collapsed. John then took over the action with a spectacular suicide, and the scene finished.

In the discussion of his exam piece that followed, Griff was asked if he had found any particular problems with the production of this play. There was a pause, and to my absolute fury, he maintained that Jay had not taken the work seriously, which had limited the scope of what he had been able to do. I let the discussion finish, then stood up in the crowded auditorium. Might I say a word or two? The tutor gave me permission to speak, so I repeated, in public, all I had previously told Griff in private.

Among the teaching staff at Central, there were many talented performers in their own right. Joe played a great jazz piano, Charles had his own one-man show in the West End and another tutor was a star in a prestigious poetry speaking group. However, the Student's Union was terribly short of money and so I asked Cliff if he could possibly come and put on an entertainment to raise funds for them. As ever, he responded at once, and to everyone's delight, he brought his guitar and gave us a wonderful evening, raising several hundred pounds for student welfare.

There was an unexpected spin-off to his visit, when we all went to the presentation of our diplomas at London University. My father's brother, Canon J.A.Douglas, had been a past Chairman of the Senate, and had often sent us a postcard, that showed him in his very impressive robes. I knew that the original picture was, supposedly, hanging in Senate House, and this occasion seemed a one-off chance to see it, and I asked one of the welcoming committee if that would be possible. He went off to investigate, but when he came back, he was very apologetic. Apparently, Uncle John's likeness had been moved to a store in the cellars, and might be difficult to find. He was terribly sorry, but would I please come to the top table, to meet the VIPs.

I was introduced as,"the niece of one of our past chairmen." It was the great non-event of the year. No-one showed the remotest interest. Then my sponsor added, "And Mrs Norris has another claim to fame...", I was intrigued and had absolutely no idea what he was going to say, "She taught Cliff Richard...". It seemed that he had, somehow, heard about the concert at Central. The result of this revelation was very dramatic, as everyone at the table was suddenly very interested. I think Uncle Johnny might have been very amused at being doubly relegated, robes and all!

The course ended, and Ernest and I organised yet another rhymed car rally for July 14th. We had, staying with us at the time, Bob and Mary's older daughter, Carole, who was a very lively, attractive sixteen year old. Her parents had sent her to stay with us, to give her an experience of life in Europe, and I had taken her with me to Central. One of the acting students had taken a great shine to her, and I was afraid he had designs on her, so I reminded him that she was only sixteen. Hands off! It was interesting to see the differences between English and American teenagers. She had lovely curly hair, used virtually no make-up, and was, what Bob called, 'au naturel'. There were slight problems, food-wise, as she had very definite likes and dislikes. Ernest was very amused when, after supper one evening, she said, "That was delicious. What was it?" I told her it was liver. She looked horrified. "Liver? I don't like liver!" We took her on holiday to Wales, where she met her admirer from Central, and we all had a great time. My year on secondment was finally over, and, in September, it was back to reality and Riversmead.

Chapter 9

There were several things to cheer me up. It was great to be with Keith again, who seemed delighted that I was back to sit next to him at school dinner, and partner him, at lunch time bridge sessions. I had fallen for the charms of a one of a litter of labrador-cross-spaniel puppies, so we had a dog. He had a lovely golden, long-haired coat and immediately adored James, who took him for walks along the bank of the New River at the back of the house. Remembering J, Alfred Prufrock, we called him Freddie.

Best news of all was that the headmaster was retiring at Christmas, and, with the staff party in mind, I wrote a parody of Noel Coward's 'I wonder what happened to him?' I remember it ended,

"From Grammar to College was the path that he trod,
And, if you consider, it does seem quite odd,
That he should end up in a Secondary Mod...
Yes, we all know what happened to him! "

And to the tune of "We've been together now...", Keith and I sang :

"He's been in teaching now for forty years
And a plaque's going up to read.
He's served his term, and now he's been released
From his sentence at Riversmead.....!"

So the term ended and the new Head arrived in January.

Back in Pine Close, change was also in the air. Ernest hated the idea of moving anywhere, but all those years with Buddy, and her itching feet, had left their mark on me. I had never lived in one house for a long time and we had been at 'Wits End' for seventeen.years. The pictures in house agents' windows were a constant temptation, and I had secretly gone round one or two properties. Past experience had shown that getting Ernest to leave his garden would be very difficult, not to mention any suggestion of taking out a new mortgage.

Nevertheless, an advertisement in the local paper looked interesting. A Georgian house nearby, with four bedrooms and a garage, was for sale at only slightly more than we could get for our house. That Saturday, I arranged a viewing at 11am, and told Ernest there was something I wanted him to see, a surprise. Still in his bedroom slippers, I got him away from the washing up, into the car and along the A10, to Churchfield Path, an unadopted road that led, finally, to the nearby parish church. The agent was waiting and showed us round. Ernest was reluctantly convinced and, after one or two setbacks, we bought it!

We had our usual debate about a name, and agreed that lines from one of T S Eliot's 'Quartets', sounded just what we hoped for, "And all shall be well, and all manner of thing shall be well....". So we called our lovely new home 'LITTLE GIDDING' , and Ernest, James, Freddie the dog, and I, moved in. Paul had started his teaching career in a residential job at Danesbury, an approved school, and was only about ten miles away. He loved the new house and had some good ideas on what we could do with the basement. There were two large rooms, one was to be my study and the other we named 'The Smugglers Cave', a room for parties.

We needed designs on the walls I had painted white, and one day, Mike, Janice's husband, came along holding a book with colourful pictures of fish. When he left, several hours later, the room was completely transformed. In an underwater world of wrecked galleons, around which swam brightly coloured tropical fish, there were wonderfully shaped rocks and trailing fronds of exotic seaweed. All I had to do was buy a few lobster pots and some old fish nets, hang them across the ceiling, add some concrete benches from the garden centre, and the party atmosphere was complete. Paul put the finishing touch, when he bought us an old fruit machine, complete with a boxful of pennies. We were to have some great parties at 'Little Gidding' over the next fifteen years.

There was a lovely big drawing room, and a separate dining room, but the kitchen was small, for such a big house. We applied for planning permission to extend it, and for a conservatory, to house our flourishing house plant collection. A flight of steps would lead down into the basement so, at a party, there would be plenty of room for the guests to circulate. Ernest made plans to organise the totally neglected garden, which had three equal areas. At the back of the house, he made triangular flowerbeds, edged with paved paths, in a circular pattern around a central bay tree. On one side, there was a sunken area with a lawn, for sunbathing and any football kicking, while on the other side, he grew some very good fruit and vegetables.

We had a low wall built in front of the house, and added wooden shutters beside the bull's-eye studded bay windows. A flight of five steps, with wrought iron hand rails, led to the yellow front door, and we bought a bold, black, lion door knocker as part of the new door furniture. There was a garage and a garden shed, which I painted in blue and white stripes, so we now were all ready to enjoy 'Little Gidding'.

At Riversmead, Bill had resigned to take charge of fund raising for 'Tear Fund', a Christian famine relief agency. I had introduced him to Cliff, originally, to answer some awkward questions on the bible, at a time when Cliff was considering joining the Jehovah's Witnesses, which would have meant giving up his show business career. They became good friends, and when Cliff decided to sell 'Rookswood', he had moved in with Bill, and his mother, Mary, in their home in Finchley. Mary was a real darling, and the arrangement worked so well that they went on to share homes, first in Totteridge, and finally in Weybridge.

One year, Cliff had been tremendously generous, inviting us to end the July 14th car rally at 'Rookswood', where he would bring in caterers to provide the refreshments. It was great fun, as the contestants all set off, not knowing where the route would end. Imagine their delight when the final instruction took them to the huge iron gates of Cliff's very impressive home. We had an unforgettable party afterwards, with delicious food and drink, and it didn't even matter that it rained!

Keith and I would miss him so, before Bill left Riversmead, for old times' sake, I wrote one last entertainment, for the three of us to perform. It was called,

'TELLY-TIME'

ALL: *There's one place in our school where the lessons don't pall,*
Where a teacher may go with no worries at all,
It's that haven of peace at the back of the hall,
With the "Programmes for Schools" on the telly.

JAY: *On those days when you feel you're not really inspired,*
KEITH: *When, with interest, the pupils don't seem to be fired,*
BILL: *Come along! Take a seat! For they never get tired*
ALL: *Of those "Programmes for Schools" on the telly.*

JAY: *On Monday, it's Nature, the birds and the bees,*
Just how little things grow with the greatest of ease,
It's quite dangerous ground, but it's certain to please,
ALL: *On the 'Programmes for Schools' on the telly.*

KEITH: *Mathematics on Tuesday is sure to amuse,*
All those interesting shapes, seen from various views,
And, with luck, you may just catch the end of the News,
ALL: *On the 'Programmes for Schools' on the telly*

BILL: *Every Wednesday it's history, with battles and war,*
And, just two weeks from now, there's a great treat in store,
It's called "Torture in Tudor Times", (just for Form Four),

ALL: *On the "Programmes for Schools" on the telly.*

JAY: *It's on Thursday, romance can be felt in the air,*
For a boy's met a girl, and they've found that they care,
Well, perhaps, one could call it a current affair?
ALL: *On the "Programme for Schools" on the telly.*

KEITH: *But the best day is Friday, that's never a flop,*
BILL: *How we bless Logie Baird, and just rate him the top,*
JAY: *For from nine until four, there is something, non-stop,*
ALL: *On those 'Programmes for Schools' on the telly!*

1970, brought a new member of staff to the English Department, and its emerging little sister, Drama, in the person of Ron, who had come from Central to do his teaching practice at Riversmead. We were so impressed with him that we offered him a job, and he accepted. Ron was tremendously likeable, and when he had problems finding somewhere to live, we offered him the study, in the basement at 'Little Gidding'. It worked very well as he was a delightful man, and it would have been impossible not to warm to someone who was so kind and thoughtful, and we all did. Best of all, he made me laugh! When he arrived I had already started work on the Easter term play, 'The Reluctant Dragon', and he was a huge help as stage manager.

He had problems, however, in his day to day teaching, particularly if a degree of confrontation was involved. He hated 'the iron fist in the velvet glove', that made the school-world go round. At the end of May, the new Head asked if the two of us, in the drama department, could run a six week leavers' course, for fifth formers to join, once their exams were over. It must keep them occupied till the end of term. I loved the idea and chose the theme, 'Play The Game', as a working title. We would include singing and choral speaking, movement and dance, as well as improvisation and acting skills. At the end of term we should aim to produce a 'show', but with the most unlikely 16 year olds, ever!

Initially, once their exams were over, some of the group, particularly the boys, had tried to 'help' the games teachers on the playing field, by sitting in the sun and watching cricket. I went out and hauled them, very reluctantly, back into the building. Ron did not approve: he felt that they should be allowed to chose what they wanted to do. He thought it would be impossible to do drama work, with non-volunteers. I didn't agree, and pointed out that we were committed to supervising the group at close quarters. They had to join us in the Hall, like it or not, and we had to catch their interest.

Once I had convinced Ron that we could break through their apathetic reluctance, the whole thing took off. They sang, they danced, they acted, they spoke poetry, and the result, to their total amazement, was a very good show, that thoroughly entertained the whole school. After the performance, they called us into a classroom where they thanked us both for making it all such fun. They frankly admitted that they hadn't wanted to join in, but were really glad we had made them, and had bought us each a little present. I was given a box of chocolates, and Ron got a cigarette lighter. We were both delighted. In July, Ron left teaching, to become the Director of Drama at Coventry Cathedral, and we only lost touch when he abandoned education altogether, and went back to a previous existence as an accountant.

Bob and Mary's son, Paul, came to stay with us in the summer holidays, as his sister had, two years earlier. He was cheerful and enthusiastic and we really liked him, but I was slightly worried, when he asked to go to a Rock Concert on the Isle of Wight. After all, he was only 16. I phoned Bob, who thought that it would be fine, so off he went. At the time, Cliff had a luxurious motor cruiser, 'Pomander' on the Thames, which slept six, and he, very generously, offered to lend it to me for a week. We had already borrowed it for a holiday on the Norfolk Broads, so I knew what a great time one could have on such a magnificent boat. Derek came down from North Wales, to take charge of the galley, as he was a superb chef, and I asked my college chums, Pam and Dennis, who knew all about boats, to come with their two young sons. Dennis was to be our Captain, with Pam as First Mate. Ernest wished us well, but asked to be excused, this time, and he missed a really wonderful voyage through the beautiful upper reaches of the Thames.

All went well, with Derek cooking super meals, and Dennis thoroughly enjoying his role as Captain. Pam and I were lower grade helpers, getting Den his daily newspaper, doing the washing up and cleaning the kitchen after Derek's efforts. Paul seemed to have fun, though he dropped his spectacles overboard and had to be physically restrained by Dennis, from jumping in after them. We all watched, as they swirled round and round, before a slow motion disappearance into the murky, fast running stream. When he went back to New York, Paul left us with a catchphrase we still use. Watching the Commonwealth Games on television, he became a very vocal, ardent supporter of, would you believe, Uganda! It was such an unlikely choice that it made a great impression on us all, and so, "Let's Go Uganda!!" is still part of our family's vocabulary.

Derek and I were both heavy smokers, and Den would, occasionally, puff on his pipe, so after we got home, I wrote a little verse:

GIVING UP THE WEED!

"I am thinking of giving up smoking,
I am going to abandon the weed,
Though my good resolutions will probably fail,
For I know, from the past, that I'm terribly frail,
Yet I feel much less healthy each time I inhale!
So I'm thinking of giving up smoking.

I just know that I ought to stop smoking,
As it's, clearly, not doing me good,
For my throat's very sore, and my cough's getting bad,
And the stains on my fingers are driving me mad,
So if I can stop puffing, I ought to be glad,
But it's miserable, giving up smoking.

Oh, it's frightfully hard to stop smoking,
And just how? Is the question you see.
I've tried sucking some sweets, but resulting from that,
I've put on several pounds in the place people pat,
So it seems I must either be kippered or fat,
But I'm sure that I should give up smoking.......and
eating.......tomorrow!

The 'Which play are you going to next year?' question had been raised in the summer term, but I hadn't really any answer. I'd already done so many productions, that the choice was becoming increasingly difficult. Then I had a brainwave! Fifteen years had passed since the 1955 'Toad of Toad Hall', and everyone who had been in it, or might have seen it, had, long since, disappeared into the bright blue yonder, except, of course, Janice and Cliff.

We had quite a lot of talent in the Dramatic Society, in particular, a boy called Andrew, who was a natural for the part of Toad. He was the House Captain of Salisbury, my House, and very good at rugby. I could see who would play Ratty, Badger and Mole, and there were several ideas from Central that I wanted to try out. On hearing that it was a guaranteed financial success, the new Head agreed my choice, so began, what I thought would be, a simple stroll down Memory Lane. As usual, it wasn't like that at all.

Andrew was every bit as good as I had thought he would be, and had a very idiosyncratic idea of the character of Toad, that was both original and highly theatrical. He was definitely the star, and then he broke his leg in a rugby match. His mother phoned to give me the news, asking if he could possibly continue in the role, otherwise all his extra curricular interests would collapse. She assured me that he would be out of plaster in six weeks, in time for our December performance. I quickly agreed, as I certainly had no-one else good enough to take the part, and offered to ferry him, by car, to and from evening rehearsals. It turned out to be well worth any effort, as he was a brilliant Toad, and an unexpected bonus was, that he had a gold front tooth, which caught the stage spotlights, and sent flashes back into the audience. I felt quite guilty when I was congratulated on introducing such an original idea.

I had been a member of NATE, The National Association of the Teachers of English, for some time, but had never gone on any of the courses they ran in the school holidays. Almost by chance, I saw an announcement in the Times Ed., that a three day stay in an Oxford college, included a talk on his work by Charles Causley, whose poems I loved. I phoned at once, and booked a place. It was really exciting for, as all the students were away on holiday, we stayed in the college building at St Edmund's Hall. I loved Oxford and the general atmosphere of academic study. Charles Causley was a very charming, rather shy man, but he was a good speaker and I learnt all about his life in Launceston, where he lived with his mother and taught in a village school. He read 'The Ballad of the Bread Man' superbly, and some poems about the local church. The others on the course were interesting and a lecturer from Nottingham took me out to tea the next day, so the whole thing was a huge success.

The following week, I was in London, with Derek, and we were going to see an Ibsen play at the Piccadilly Theatre. We went into a nearby pub, to have a pre-theatre drink, and there, sitting at the bar, was Charles Causley. I rushed over to him and put my hand on his shoulder, "How wonderful to see you," I said. He looked taken aback. He couldn't think who on earth I was. "I'm sorry," he began, "but.." Then, of course, I realised that, though, to me, he was someone I felt I knew well, to him, I was a total stranger. I was horribly embarrassed, and apologised profusely, but once he saw what had happened, we chatted about the Oxford course, and how good it had been. Derek couldn't resist being very amused by the whole thing.

Now that Drama was part of the main school curriculum, I had done some 'pot-hunting', to try to give it academic respectability in the eyes of the outside world. From Central, I had the (London University Certificate in Diction and Drama), LUCDD, plus Central's own CSD. I took the exams for an LGSM, Licentiate of the Guildhall School of Speech and Drama, and an ACP, Associate of the College of Preceptors. They were all pretty meaningless in terms of practical teaching, but the letters looked good in the school's prospectus the new Head had introduced. The ACP even gave me the right to wear a gown, with a hood, to impress the parents and show that Drama really was a proper subject, to be taken seriously, for an exam. I had hoped the Head was suitably impressed.

I found out what he really thought, almost by accident. Thanks to Cliff's fund raising, we had been able to convert a classroom into the Richard Drama Studio. It had everything, including blackout curtains, stage lanterns and wall to wall carpeting. I was in the middle of a lesson when the Head appeared with a very presentable young chap in tow. He introduced the newcomer, and said that he would be joining the English Department. The Head then spoke the words that were, perhaps, the greatest putdown of my life. "He'd like to do some drama. You show him. He'll soon pick it up!" So much for academic excellence. By a real stroke of luck, that young man was Charlie, who was to be very successful in the future, both as a colleague and as a close friend. Drama, from then on, became a thriving department of two.

Chapter 10

Hertfordshire, under John Newsom, had been in the forefront of the introduction of CSE, the new Certificate of Secondary Education, and we had been involved in the running of some of the pilot schemes, including one in Oral English. There were several positive effects in the new comprehensive schools. The range of ability, in pupils taking an exam, was considerably widened and it allowed most subjects to be assessed by a test of one kind or another. In Drama, examination panels were set up, ideas were exchanged, and an agreed syllabus emerged. There would be standardisation sessions and then we would examine, in tandem, with the school's own drama teacher. It seemed to be a sensible scheme, and it worked very well in practice

Every pupil had to be in a piece of theatre they had personally initiated. They could be advised and helped by the teacher, but that was all. A 'Grade 1' should be a difficult target to reach, and after the performance aspect, there would be an oral, to be sure that there was an understanding of the whole project. A fairly brief diary should record workshop sessions and theatre visits to show an appreciation of dramatic purpose. We had set our shoulders to the wheel!

Because every candidate had their own piece of theatre, no group could have more than fifteen members. There just would not be time to deal with more than fifteen single productions, and the drama option was hugely oversubscribed, as many as fifty wanting to join each year. Obviously, there were two groups, a 4th year and a 5th year, so I was very busy, as there were also first, second and third year lessons for the rest of the school, plus some English teaching. Charlie had come at just the right time!

I had wanted to start each fourth year drama group with a theatre visit and we settled on an overnight stay in Stratford-upon Avon, as being the most exciting option in every way. We could all fit into the school minibus, which I had often driven, and there were plenty of inexpensive B & Bs where we could stay, in the popular tourist town. A tour of the Shakespeare Properties, like Ann Hathaway's Cottage and Mary Arden's House, would fill the gaps in historical knowledge that were sure to arise, and. finally we would see a Shakespeare play, wonderfully acted, in an exciting auditorium. The Head agreed that we could have two days off and everyone paid up.

We had decided to split into single sex groups for the boarding houses, with Charlie and eight boys in one, and the seven girls with me, next door. It sounded trouble free! That first night, I saw the girls into the two family rooms they had been given, tucked them up in bed and went to my room, at the end of the corridor, for a well-earned rest. We had seen a wonderful production of 'A Comedy of Errors', Charlie had taken the boys next door, and, tomorrow, we would be spending a fascinating day, in one of my favourite towns. Everything was going to plan.

It was about an hour later, after I had put my book down and turned out the light, that I heard faint whispers and giggles from the other end of the corridor. Sleepily, I got out of bed and went to investigate. I tried the girls' door. It was locked. All was deadly silent. I rattled the handle and told them I knew they were awake and I wanted the door open, IMMEDIATELY. The door opened and there, huddled in various corners, were our boys. Furiously I ushered them downstairs, anxious not to wake the landlady, a Miss Williams, who would have been very shocked. By the time I had got the boys back into their house, and closed the front door quietly, the girls were already back in bed and pretending to be asleep.

In the morning we gathered in our sitting room, for a post mortem. Charlie was amazed and had not heard a sound of the midnight exodus. I was keen to be sure that nothing like that would ever happen again, and for them all to realise that I would not be telling the Head, because it might reflect badly on the good reputation of the group, affecting future drama visits. I told them off first, and then said, "I shall not report this to the Headmaster; why do you think that is?" There was a pause and then one of the girls said, "Because you'd get into trouble!" Charlie and I had considerable difficulty in keeping straight faces.

The next major happening at Riversmead, was, in a way, connected with Stratford-upon-Avon. The previous Head had once suggested that our school play should, "aim to raise the cultural level of the district", whereas I thought a school production should be, primarily, something that the pupils could do well, extending them to produce good results, in a piece of drama they understood and everyone enjoyed. Certainly, I did not expect to direct a Shakespeare play at the school in 1974.

It all started with Cliff, as many good things seemed to at the time. He came to see me with a request. Could he come back and be in another play? When I realised that he was serious, I told him that, sadly, it was not possible. When he wanted to know why, I reminded him of the many hours we had rehearsed for the numerous productions he had been involved in at school. He was now a successful pop star, in great demand and he lived some distance away from Cheshunt. My minimum preparation time for a play had always been three months, which had never seemed to be too long. Time was against the idea; there simply wouldn't be enough.

With great charm and tact, Cliff proceeded to demolish my objections. It did not matter how long it took; he would be available. His pop singing career could be put on hold. Getting to rehearsals would be easy as he had a car. He was really convincing, and I promised to look into what might be possible, and let him know. There were certainly a great many pros to set against the cons. Whatever we did, it would be good PR for the school, even if we didn't succeed in raising the cultural level of the district.

It was a very tempting offer, but, first, I had to choose a play, and look at the various options for getting the right cast to be in it. We had tried the staff-pupil combination of actors in 'The Heartless Princess', twenty-five years earlier, but we had never invited old pupils to join in as well, and Cliff was, when all was said and done, a past pupil. Then what about past members of staff, like Sue? The show could be a get-together for the whole clan, and there was a timely, twenty-fifth anniversary coming up, as Cheshunt County Secondary School had started in the huts on the playing fields in 1949.

The play was the thing. Could I try a Shakespeare? On our very first date, when I was seventeen, Ernest and I had gone to see 'A Midsummer Night's Dream', at the Open Air Theatre, in Regent's Park. I had loved it, with the moths circling round the spotlights and Mendelssohn's wonderful overture, competing with the birds, to make a truly romantic evening. I had seen it many times since and, at Trent Park, we had acted an excerpt, the Artisans' Play, for a college Open Day presentation. I had played 'Bottom', thoroughly enjoying the comedy romp in Pyramus and Thisbe.

For a school production, we needed a big cast and MSND had one. I could see Cliff as Oberon, elegant and charming, surrounded by our prettiest first year girls as fairies. I spent some time studying the text, and realised that the play would easily divide into four separate rehearsal groups, with pupils as the lovers and the fairies, and past pupils and staff as the court and the artisans. I went to see what the Head thought and he loved the idea. Finally, we would be up there with the cultural elite!

I met Cliff to talk through the practicalities, and gave him a choice of role. He could play elegant, charming Oberon, like falling off a log, or would he like a challenge? Rough peasant comedy might be harder, but Bottom was a gem of a part: which? He didn't hesitate: he chose Bottom.

In a strange way, everything else fell into place. Cliff's choice of part had given me a wonderful chance to re-unite some of the 1955 cast of 'Toad' and, after a few auditions, we had our whole cast and all we needed was an introductory 'hugging' session to set the ball rolling. Back in the late sixties, just after Central, I had met Derek, a Senior Drama Advisor from North Wales. He ran a Youth Theatre group and when I needed someone special to run an introductory Drama weekend workshop for MSND, there could be no-one better. To my delight he agreed to come, and to bring his assistant advisor, Dave, with him.

In no time at all, it seemed, the drama weekend was upon us. It was actors only, and there were thirty-eight of them, with ages ranging from twelve to the mid-forties. Very few of the cast really knew more than one or two of the others and the buzz of getting to know a real live pop star was tremendously exciting. I was sure that Cliff would be fine. It was the present pupil contingent that I was slightly worried about. It was all up to Derek and Dave, and, of course, they turned up trumps. The introductory warm-up, was a WOW!

The very first exercise set the tone. Everyone had to walk around the stage on their own, but if they made a physical contact with anyone else, they were stuck to that person. Within about one minute, Cliff had little girls stuck all over his arms and his back. It was wonderfully ridiculous and we all landed up in hysterics. On a more serious note, there were trust exercises, and work on voice and movement. It was a bonding process, exactly what was needed and we planned a final visit from Derek at the end of June.

For the last piece of the jigsaw, we needed a talented art director. Janice's Mike, was, other than Ken, by far the best artist and stage designer I had ever met, so I was over the moon when, despite his busy schedule as a teacher of art, he said he would join us. At the time, I was very keen on paper sculpture, and I wanted to avoid having a set for 'A Midsummer Night's Dream' that was a conventional forest, painted on the backdrop. Mike agreed, and even did a rough sketch of how the ass's head might look in paper. No longer was it a pantomime donkey, but a beautiful, elegant, unicorn-like creature, the ass as seen in a dream, through Titania's drugged eyes.... "What angel wakes me from my flowery bed?"... So 'DREAMS', became the central theme that ran through everything we did.

Charlie thought it would be exciting if we had a super, deluxe programme, and offered to take responsibility for getting it organised. This would not be easy, as money would have to be raised, through carefully chosen advertising, to offset the cost of printing. Keith would take photographs of everyone in the cast, and I suggested that each of them should tell Charlie their 'dream' for the future.

The programme was very impressive, on A4 glossy white card cover, with gold lettering. It gave the dates of the seven performances , starting on Wednesday, 3rd July, and there were photos of the members of the cast, each with a summary of their personal 'dream'. There was a very relaxed picture of Cliff, in a polo-necked sweater, and it was no surprise to learn that his dream was to 'play Heathcliff in a musical adaptation of Wuthering Heights'. Twenty-two years were to pass, before he got his wish. The other dreams varied from the sublime to the ridiculous. Janice wanted to 'see Venice before it sank', while Brian, (Badger in 'Toad'), dreamt of being 'a professional gambler'. I wondered if his wife knew?!

The main advertisers, carefully chosen, were given a quote from the play to preserve the Shakespearian connection. My friend, Curly, a bespoke tailor, with a very upmarket clientele, had 'Get your apparel together', and Cheshunt Travel did even better with 'What revels are in hand?... How shall we beguile the lazy time if not with some delight?' My favourite quote, however, was the one chosen by Longman's, the publisher of 'The Group Approach to Shakespeare', 'Bless thee Bottom! Bless thee, thou art translated'.

I had written a producer's note at the back, saying that we had approached the play as an extended dream, and Richard, the music director, explained his use of 'La Volta' by William Byrd, in the incidental music. Finally, on the last page, we summarised the plot of the play, the history of the school, and an impressive list of past productions. I glowed with pride. It was all terribly exciting.

Work on the production had started straight away, and everyone had been given a schedule of when they would be needed. It all had to be done outside school hours, so nearly every evening, and most weekends, were affected. To my relief, the rehearsals were very enjoyable, and almost all the cast took to Shakespeare, like ducks to water. Lines were learnt accurately and our concentration on good drama over the years, paid off. Cliff and the other artisans renewed their old bonhomie, and, at times, I felt that they were back in my form, in Room 9.

Naturally, the media had discovered what we were up to, and word had spread as far as Sweden, so we got requests for tickets from overseas fans. ITV sent a camera crew and I was interviewed, during a 'rehearsal', for an evening chat programme. Our box office manager, who was a mathematician, had matters well in hand, tickets were printed, and we were, clearly going to play to packed houses. The costumes were almost ready, the paper sculpture in place and the make-up teams trained. Mike had made a wonderful ass's head, which looked great, though Cliff had to be careful , as it was quite awkward to keep it straight, and it looked slightly odd if Bottom's head was skew-whiff.

I wanted to open the play with a masked ball at the court, and there was an Elizabethan dance to learn. I phoned Derek, and he told me not to worry, as he was bringing Molly, a dance expert, to the final workshop. I was extremely relieved. Cliff had recorded lines from the play about dreaming, which would echo across the stage as the lights came up. We were very nearly ready for the final workshop.

Molly, slim and vivacious, turned out to be an absolute genius. From a group of non-dancers, she produced a breathtaking result that could have won a competition. The elegance and poise of the first Elizabethans, was miraculously conjured up in the school hall, to the strains of Byrd's 'La Volta'. The fairies soon learnt how to pick up Cliff, wearing the ass's head, and, despite my worst fears, they didn't drop him. At the dress rehearsal, they carried him, shoulder high, across the stage, and it almost looked as if they were flying. Cliff was very good at keeping his body rigid, as he was lifted high into the air on sixteen little arms, undoubtedly, the ultimate trust exercise. Titania looked startlingly beautiful, as she followed the procession, and the whole thing had a real magic about it.

We had struck lucky with Puck, who was mischievous but thoroughly endearing, and Oberon, very handsome, with a magnificent physique, that his scanty costume showed to great advantage! Janice and Sue were towers of strength and gave good support to Theseus, while the lovers innocently yearned and sighed, as their elders and the Duke, and magic flowers, directed. Of course, the artisans' play was brilliantly done, and the romp of Pyramus and Thisbe, the play within the play, was side splitting. Cliff gave a starring performance as Bottom, that had heart as well as laughs. He was very good indeed.

A wonderful round that I had learnt at Central, would end the play, with the stage gradually filling for the final curtain, as one by one, the four groups came on from the wings, singing. "Dona Nobis Pacem", Give Us Peace. The round format produced an impressive harmonic effect and they all sang superbly under Richard's expert tuition. The Hall would ring to the rafters with the audience's enthusiastic appreciation. Every seat was sold and we knew that we had a success on our hands. We planned to enjoy it to the full

Chapter 11

I had been very busy all day, on Sunday, June 30th. We were having the final dress rehearsal, so that we would have two clear days, before the opening night, to tie up any loose ends. We had started work in the morning at ten, and I got back to 'Little Gidding', reasonably pleased, but very tired, at about six. I had just sat down when the phone rang. It was Keith's flatmate, and he had some disturbing news. He feared that Keith might be having a recurrence of the serious heart problem, that had hospitalised him two years earlier. Could I come round and see what I thought? Of course I could, and when I saw Keith, lying on the settee in his sitting room, I was extremely worried. He looked gaunt and ill, and my first thought was that we should call his doctor immediately. He flatly refused. Nothing would induce him to risk having to spend another spell in hospital.

His friend saw me to the door, and I urged him to get the doctor, despite Keith's objections, as things could get considerably worse during the night. He clearly took note of the warning for, about an hour later, the phone rang to let me know that Keith was in the Cottage Hospital, just opposite his flat. It was after visiting hours, but I went straight round to see him. He looked a little better, tucked up neatly in a hospital bed, and I joked with him about taking an unearned rest. I never saw him again.

When I arrived at school on Monday morning, the Head called me into his office, with the news that Keith had suffered a massive heart attack during the night, and he was dead. He was only 47. I was, literally, overwhelmed with sadness. I had lost my dearest friend. We had lived in each other's pockets for nearly twenty-two years, and I couldn't imagine life at Riversmead without him. At this point, the cliché, "The show must go on", proved to be totally true. Everyone was devastated by the news, but we all knew that we must not allow our grief to affect our commitment to the success of 'The Dream'.

The performances sailed by on cloud nine. Masses of backstage visits from friends, especially for Cliff, and huge excitement every night as the curtain went up. It was wonderful to be a part of this particular dream. The 'end of the show' party came on Sunday, 14th July, my birthday. We were all exhausted, but delighted with the huge success of the production. Everyone who had worked to ensure that success, came, and the school dining room made a good venue. There was a delicious meal, cooked by the canteen staff, and the drinks were either an 'Ass's Head' a lemonade punch for the under 16s, or, with the addition of some of my very alcoholic homemade lemon wine, an 'Ass's Head with a Kick', for the rest of us. I was very moved when I was presented with a beautiful silver salver, engraved with lines from the play, "Our true intent is. All for your delight." Janice told me, later, that the jeweller had queried the punctuation. I can confidently say that I had, truly, delighted in the whole experience.

Of course, amid all this turmoil, normal life had to continue. The summer school holidays came and went, and, as the new term started, I was conscious that I had given Charlie very little real support in the actual teaching of drama. We had talked together, of course, but he had not been able to "pick it up" from practical experience, because, fairly predictably, my free periods never coincided with his drama teaching commitment, or the other way round. The various publishers' representatives, who brought books into the staff room, confirmed that there was absolutely nothing on the market covering the teaching of educational drama. There were, they assured me, plenty of very good collections of play-reading scripts, but it seemed there was little else. I asked the rep from Longmans, if he thought his company might be interested in publishing something to fill the gap. He suggested that I contact his editorial office, and they would , very probably be quite enthusiastic about the idea. He gave me a phone number. The English editor was very pleasant but non-committal. He suggested that I should write down a brief synopsis of what I had in mind, and send it to him, and we left it at that.

So far, it had all been fairly simple but now that I was faced with the reality of putting pen to paper, things seemed slightly less straightforward. I had to think exactly what such a publication ought to cover. I needed to talk to someone who actually knew what was involved in the teaching of educational drama in secondary schools. I have always enjoyed working in tandem and, at Central, some of the most interesting chats about teaching method, had been with Michael, during our lunchtime meanders around Swiss Cottage. He was a natural lateral thinker, which I, definitely, was not, and would turn things around in his mind to consider every aspect of the subject under discussion. I was a jumper to a quick conclusion, and on to the next thing. The combination was quite good. He tried to slow me down and I was keen to hurry him on. I wondered if he might be interested in joining me in a publication on the teaching of drama.

I rang Michael that evening, and he agreed to come to Cheshunt for the weekend, so that we could talk it through. Once we had had our first meeting, I knew we could do it. We were both full of ideas from Central, but as practising classroom teachers, we were clear what would or wouldn't work. What we could offer, was a practical course of drama lessons, based on sound educational principles. We drew up a synopsis of suggestions we felt teachers, new to drama, would appreciate, and it seemed pretty obvious that complete lesson plans would be very useful, with each having an introduction to the session, a development and a conclusion. Then there were drama games, one of Michael's specialities, speech and drama skills, including work on voice that I was especially keen on, and what to do if things went wrong. But how would a 'book' work? If the teacher could not easily find the information quickly, for the next lesson, it would be useless. Why not have work cards? They could be in a ring binder and it would be easy to find what was needed.

I wrote to the publisher, putting forward our suggestions, and though they approved the contents, they hated the idea of cards. For commercial reasons, they liked sets of books; they were used to books; books sold well; teachers preferred books; cards would be expensive, and so on. However, by this time, we had decided it was cards or nothing, so they accepted defeat, and cards it had to be.

It is really exciting to see your name in print, for the right reason. "JAY NORRIS, Head of the Drama Department at Riversmead School, Cheshunt and MICHAEL EVANS, Head of the Communications Department at Deeside Senior High School" didn't sound like us, but it was. Our very first publication, "DRAMA RESOURCE CARDS", with a dedication to Philip, our tutor at Central, came out in 1977, and sold well, running to a fourth impression in 1984. Sadly, when Longmans wanted us to do some more work for them, things had changed. Michael was tremendously busy at school and the meetings we would need, which involved him driving all the many miles down to Cheshunt, were very time-consuming, and virtually impossible. I quite understood the problems of long-distance collaboration so there were no hard feelings.

Several years later, we actually did do a little more writing together. Philip, from Central, was asked by British Telecom to be their Santa Claus and read the 'Christmas Stories for Children', over the phone. He had just the right voice, but absolutely no desire to write the actual stories, so he asked me if I could be persuaded to do it. It would pay peanuts, but it sounded an extremely interesting challenge, so I agreed. I liked Philip, and certainly owed him a debt of gratitude, for many of the drama ideas we had used in 'Drama Resource Cards'.

BT wanted ten stories, and when I thought about it, that seemed a lot to write in a very limited time. It crossed my mind that, if I could get Michael to undertake five of them, it would be much more fun, and, to my great relief, he gallantly agreed to come to my rescue. We decided to try to find a style that would make them all seem to have been written by one person, and I offered to have a go at the first one, to see how it went.

The parameters set by BT were fairly stringent. The stories had to last for exactly two minutes, when read by Santa, and they must have a clear narrative line, with a beginning, a middle and an end. They should be aimed at five to seven year olds, and make the callers keen to hear

Father Christmas's next telephone story. Of course, they had to appeal, equally, to both boys and girls, and should, definitely, keep in mind the peace and goodwill themes of the Christmas season. It was not easy, but I settled on a story about a little lost puppy, which would, hopefully, be a sure fire winner.

When Michael's turn came, he had some fascinating ideas. There was Tim, for whom all the toys in the shop came alive, and then the brilliant introduction of an obnoxious elf called Nowty, who was the villain of the piece, and tried poor Santa's patience to the limit. Nowty may have been grumpy and careless, but, magically, everything would always come right in the end, and he gave an edge to some of the stories that made them exciting and unpredictable.

I went on to write about, among others, good little Chloe, who saved a bedraggled Christmas Tree Fairy from disaster, and the naughty twins, Nigel and Nicky, who rescued a poor old tramp from certain hypothermia. All with very happy endings, and only taking exactly two minutes for Santa to read. Philip was pleased with our efforts and made a very good job of reading the stories aloud, even managing a specially gruff voice for Nowty. We were, however, never told how many calls were made on Santa's hotline, so the reaction of the paying customers remained a mystery.

The 1970s were also proving to be a very interesting time at home. 'Little Gidding' was quite a big house and we had plenty of space, as Paul was now teaching at Mount St Mary's, a Jesuit College near Chesterfield. Towards the end of the '75 football season, the local paper in Cheshunt, had appealed for somewhere for one of the Spurs players to stay for two weeks. Paul suggested that we could easily offer to help, and James, a very keen Spurs fan, enthusiastically gave his support.

I was not keen on the idea, because I taught all day, and the thought of extra cooking, plus caring for a, possibly dreary, footballer did not sound an attractive proposition. Ernest thought it might be interesting, but left it to me to decide. In the end, emotional blackmail worked, and I agreed, so we phoned the Tottenham office with our offer which they immediately accepted. John arrived, with a suitcase, two hours later

From the programme for 'A Midsummer Night's Dream'
at Riversmead in 1974.

"Cliff's dream is that he will play Heathcliff in a musical adaptation of 'Wuthering Heights'."

'Buddy'
The district nurse in Enfield in 1949.

'Ratty and Badger'
in 'Toad of Toad Hall' 1956.

With Jill and Michael at the Central School of Speech and Drama 1968.

At Riversmead in 1974 'A Midsummer Night's Dream' with Art Director Mike.

First School Cruise with Bill and Keith in St Mark's Square, Venice.

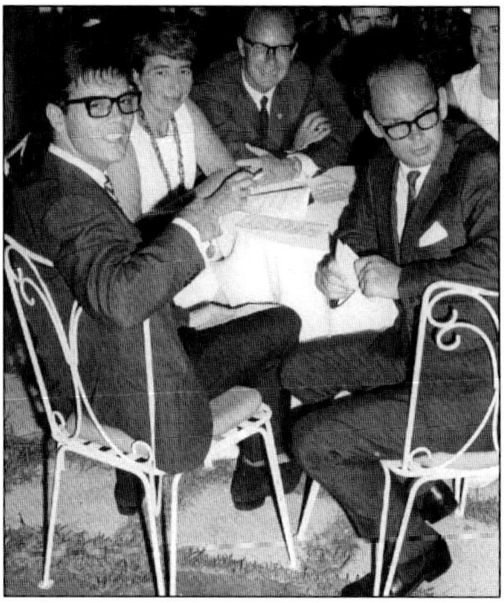

At the Governor's Mansion in Madeira 2nd School Cruise.

'The Grils' with Paul.

Ernest

With John our first footballer

My Retirement Party
at Riversmead.

After the Gospel
Concert in Harrogate.
'I'm very sorry madam
but we do not accept
North Yorkshire
Library Cards'.

Breakfast at the Quinta in Portugal. Ali, Giles, Paul, Jay, Bob, Mike

With Paul and James at Beverley Races for 'The Ernest Norris Memorial Handicap'

Backstage at the Albert Hall with Nicky, Jan, Mike, Nigel

At 'Charters' with Gloria for Cliff's 60th birthday party.

Cliff with Toad!

In Mike and Jan's garden for his 60th birthday.

A dinner party at Furlong House in York.
Giles, Ali, Charlie, Jan, Mike, Nicky, Nigel.

School Friends
'The Young Ones'

Cliff and Jan at
'The Barge'.

In Barbados with Cliff
and Bernard.

The Queen Mary 2

Aboard The Queen Mary 2
in 2010 with Bernard the
Cunard Commodore.

"My Life My Way" – The Barge
Signing Oct 2008

a handsome, charming, intelligent man, he was not at all what I had expected. He had been spotted by a football talent scout, while he was still at school. but his father had insisted that he should go to college, in case the football career did not come to anything, and he had qualified as a games teacher. From Dundee a transfer had taken him to Spurs, and as soon as the season ended, he was getting married. We all liked him, and I think he was quite impressed by our social life, as we had Cliff coming to supper that very evening!

In the two weeks that followed, I realised that I knew absolutely nothing about the life of a professional footballer. At best, they only have a brief career, and, even that, can be cut short by injury. I saw that football was quite a pleasant way of earning a living, and not a matter of life and death. However, once when John was very tense before a match, I reminded him that it was, after all, only a game. He replied, in a strong Scottish accent, in a phrase we still use, if someone doesn't take something seriously enough, "It's no a gamer Scrar-ble!" John's two weeks were soon over, and, as we really liked him, we were very pleased that, coming back for the following season, he brought his lovely new wife to meet us.

That looked like the end of our football-guest experiment, and we were just settling back to normality, when the Spurs office called. Was there a vacancy at our house, now that John had left? Another Scot, this time from Aberdeen, urgently needed somewhere to live. I said we would let them know, and immediately phoned John to find out what he thought. John played as a forward, and the new prospect was a defender, so they had often confronted each other on the football field. John was, predictably, rather doubtful, but I had just put the phone down, when the front door bell rang. It was Willie, and when I saw him, I was sure he would fit in very well. He was also a charmer, tall, slim and elegant, with lovely reddy-gold, curly hair, and of course, blue eyes. He moved in immediately and stayed for the next six months.

Willie was a card player, and so was I. I would arrive back from school to find him sitting at our card table, shuffling a deck and saying, "What'll I beat you at now, then?" I showed him how to play 'Bezique', and he taught us a very good game, 'O Hell!', that the Spurs played on long coach journeys. He also enjoyed 'Scrabble'. One day I lost to him, and let out a gasp of mock horror, that I, an English teacher, had been beaten by a FOOTBALLER! Willie smiled, "Aye, but a footballer with five O levels!" Finally, he bought a house in Hoddesdon, and his attractive wife, Lynda, came to join him in the south. She had just had their second child, a lovely baby girl, Victoria. Their little son, Stephen, was absolutely delightful, and gave us yet another addition to our family sayings, asking if he could have another 'BIKSKIT'.

One unexpected advantage that came with our guest footballers, was that we could sometimes have seats in the directors' box, at home games, with drinks, at half time, in the players' lounge. At school, the Spurs supporters I taught were green with envy, the Arsenal fans, white with fury. The best thing of all was that we had made some interesting new additions to my Wall of Friendship.

Chapter 12

In 1979, Charlie decided to do the Central CSD Course, so, sadly, I lost his cheerful support for a whole year, but I was really pleased for him, as I knew he would have a very absorbing and stimulating time at Swiss Cottage. The Christmas parties had stopped, because a group of new staff wanted to have a disco instead, so I only wrote the odd verse or two, to amuse myself. In 1971, when the currency change came in, I made-up a rhyme that began like this:

MONEY!

Oh, they're giving us decimal coinage,
so it's farewell to old L.S.D.,
Now we're being converted we mustn't be dense,
To be hopeless at adding is just no defence,
And five pence to a shilling? Well, you know it makes sense,
Now we're getting that decimal Coinage

......and so on.......

And, later, another in a similar rhyme pattern,

HOLIDAYS

Oh, we're going in search of the sun,
For to travel abroad seems such fun,
They all say that hotel, in the old part of town,
Is exactly the place, if you want to get brown
And have lots of fresh air, for the roof's falling down!
Still we're probably going abroad.

Yes, it's marvellous flying away,
To that island with palms round the bay,
You can go on a tour, and see all of the sights,
Or engage in an orgy of foreign delights,
Why, on earth, do they call it,"ten days, with eight nights"?
Yes, it's interesting flying abroad.

You can go on a cruise, so we're told,
Get away from the rain and the cold,
With no licensing hours, and the booze duty free,
And the ship rolling on in the swell of the sea,
We're afraid all you'll want, is a nice cup of tea!
It's a wonderful life on a cruise.

.......etc....etc......!

Holidays have always played an important part in my life, and I have been thoroughly spoilt, by going on various enjoyable visits. When James was a baby, we stayed with Pam and Den, at their lovely home in Saltwood, which was great fun, as their little son Mick-Micks was a mere ten days older. We went to see Paul in Switzerland, when he was at Lycée Jacquard, and then there were the various tours of Wales with Bob and Mary's children, when they came to Europe. Ernest loved racing at Deauville, so northern France, with the added attraction of the Normandy beaches and the Bayeux tapestry, was always a must. School cruises had given me a few glimpses of Italy, but I had never been to Rome. The Christmas holidays in 1979, seemed just the right time to remedy that omission, so we went to Cheshunt Travel at The Pond, and booked a ten day package.

We were to fly to Rome and stay at the Hotel de la Ville, just at the top of the Spanish Steps. At the time, Paul was teaching in a Jesuit college, so he had been able to get us tickets for midnight mass in St Peter's, and even better, a chance to see the Pope at close quarters, at one of the special public audiences. It seemed a wonderful opportunity to take a close look at the glories of the Eternal City, and at the very charismatic, Pope John Paul the second.

I had read several biographies of John Keats, with the story of his last days in the house on the Spanish Steps, so I was especially thrilled that we were staying close by. When we arrived at the hotel, its elegance was rather faded, but it was perfectly comfortable. The traffic in Rome seemed life-threatening. Cars were parked at random, regardless of any prohibition notices or lack of available spaces. Double parking on narrow, medieval streets was commonplace and, the chaotic result was phlegmatically accepted as the status quo. I was very glad that we could walk to the main attractions, but Paul decided that we had to have a car ourselves, to protect us from mad Italian motorists!

First, of course, we went to Keats' house. It was so sad. The stark emptiness of his room hit me. He had lain on that bed, looking at that ceiling, waiting to die. His friend had gone to inspect the Protestant cemetery so that he could tell the poet what it was like. When he heard of the purple violets, spreading across the graves, like a beautiful coverlet, Keats said that he felt that he could lie, at peace, under them. We visited the grave, and there they were, the soft, velvety, purple flowers. I shall never forget them.

Rome was memorably beautiful, despite the traffic, and sights like the great historic buildings and the superb ceiling in the Sistine Chapel were wonderful, yet somehow familiar, because we had so often seen pictures of them. We had often watched the Pope on TV, but nothing had prepared us for the reality of this tall, handsome man, dressed in full papal regalia, with the charm and presence of a film star.

To be able to go to midnight mass, on Christmas Eve, in St Peter's in Rome, was really special, and the little frisson of applause that ran round the congregation, when the Pope came to the altar, to begin the service, took us by surprise. In a way, it seemed out of keeping with the simplicity of the baby Jesus in his crib, the celebrant more important than the occasion. To go to an actual audience, albeit with about two thousand others, was spectacular, and we blessed the Jesuits who had got Paul the tickets.

In the large hall, there was a roped off passageway down the middle, so everyone gathered on either side, to get as close as possible to the star of the occasion. There were several priests, quite a lot of nuns and a few people in uniforms of one kind or another. All the rest, seemed like us, to be tourists. When the Pope came in he got a pop star reception, with very enthusiastic clapping, and little cheers of approval. The nuns all glowed with admiration, and John Paul was, certainly, a very impressive figure, standing head and shoulders above the clerics who surrounded him He walked down the centre of the hall, ripples of applause following him, and when he got to us, he stopped. I thought he was going to say something, but, no, he just looked over the top of my head, straight at Paul. Seconds later he moved on, but it was a very strange encounter. We had hired a car, so we were also able to go to the races, and see something of the area around the city. All in all it was a lovely way to spend Christmas.

There had been several major staffing changes at Riversmead in the seventies. Another new headmaster came, who quickly made my friend, Dave, his deputy. I thought it was a very well-earned promotion, so, just for fun, I put pen to paper once more.

SALUTE TO A NEW DEPUTY HEADMASTER

O, there's little that's good to be said for the job of a Deputy Head,
In the Admin, his room isn't what one would choose,
For it's right by the door of the Staff ladies' loos,
The 'unfashionable end', is the phrase one might use!
Yes, there's little that's good to be said,
For promotion to Deputy Head.

And some battles will always be lost, as a Deputy finds to his cost.
There's the case of young Dule, who is rather bizarre,
And was found 'drunk-in-charge', but he'd gone a bit far,
For the vehicle he'd nicked was the Headmaster's car!
Yes, some battles will always be lost,
There are cabers that just can't be tossed.

For a Deputy must be a man, who is willing to carry the can.
Now if Wayne, who's been caned, (he's a violent lad),
Arrives the next day with a sixteen stone dad,
One must smile........ and then say "So you've come, I AM glad!"
For a Deputy must be a man,
Who will duck when the sh.... hits the fan!

One is constantly put on the spot, that's a Deputy's permanent lot.
There is someone who's waiting for you, and you fear
It's that woman, who'd talk the hind leg off a deer,
Stick a note on your door, ... "ONLY FRENCH SPOKEN HERE"
One is constantly put on the spot,
So, then just "parlez francais"! Why not?

I was slightly surprised when, after the Senior Mistress retired, I was asked to put my hat in the ring for the job. I had been Head of Upper School for two years, working with Dick, the Head of Remedial Studies, and we made a good team. I liked him tremendously, as he was a very attractive man, a wonderfully cheerful disciplinarian, barely needing to raise an eyebrow to get full confessions volunteered by the culprits. He also organised any NAS/UWT union matters, and, from him, I learnt the meaning of the phrase, 'a spontaneous motion from the floor'! When he finally met Ernest, I was careful to see they didn't talk politics!

Essentially, the thing I enjoyed most about school, was the actual, hands-on teaching, and really had no desire to join the admin block high flyers. I remembered writing 'A life of headship's not a happy one', and just how true it had seemed. Of course, things were different now, there was a new headmaster, and Dave was the deputy. The fact that the salary was better was a plus, for though I was not thinking of retiring, that would make a difference to my final pension. So, in the end, I duly applied and was appointed Senior Mistress.

The new Head told me that his predecessor, in his report on members of staff, had said I was eccentric. How ridiculous! I was a happily married Tory voter, a home owner, with two children, Convent school educated, worked hard, and I had only had two days off in twenty plus years. Eccentric? Moi?

The head of English resigned in '78, and to my surprise, my sister's son, Giles, rang me at home. He wanted to know how I would feel if he applied for the vacancy. The answer was simple. I would be delighted. Despite the fact that Peggy and I had never got on well together, I had warmed to her son. His father had been a great friend, and Giles looked very like him. As he grew up, our contacts were minimal. We had played several tennis 'matches', which he always won very easily, and I knew that, after university, he had become a very good teacher of English. He was interested in the theatre, and had, recently, directed a play at the London boys' school, where he taught. It was, I had heard, necessary for some of the cast to have very short hair, so he'd had his cut, to show solidarity with them. He was my kind of chap.

I let the Head know that a close relative would be among the applicants for the Head of English post, and added that at least I could say that he would do the job well, as the work ethic in our family is, thanks to Buddy, very Victorian, and slacking is never an option. All went as planned, and, after the interview, the Head told me that Giles had been an outstanding candidate, and my recommendation had not even been a factor!

I had only accepted the post of Senior Mistress, when it was agreed that I could continue with a full teaching timetable. I definitely did not want an office in the admin block, and if I had to interview parents or children, the stage green room would do very nicely as a base. More of a problem was trying to stay as a member of the staffroom community. I made a resolution that I would NEVER, under any circumstances, use anything that happened there, to carry tales or gossip to the Head, and I tried to make sure that everyone knew this. It was harder getting the new headmaster to stop using titles like the 'Senior Management Committee', for meetings that involved him, the two deputies and me. I called us 'The Gang of Four'. It took time, but when, one day, he asked me to arrange a meeting for "The Gang of Four", I knew that the battle had been won.

Chapter 13

Giles's appointment, as head of English, made a huge improvement to my quality of life at Riversmead. He was very interested in drama, and did not see it, either as a rival subject or as a spin-off, that rightly belonged under the aegis of his department. I set out to work closely with him, and in the course of my efforts, considerably improved my own teaching skills, and made a long-term close friend. I also had a lot of fun!

I can't think of a better way of earning a living, than one where the work is so enjoyable that you would do it for nothing, and, in essence, that's what our CSE drama group lessons often turned out to be. There would be a genuine sigh of disappointment, when the end-of-lesson bell rang. We had two groups, each with about fifteen students, so running them together, with the two of us team teaching, worked well. We had an agreed system, whereby, after I had started the session with a relaxation introduction, we would begin the main topic with our 'box and cox' technique. Whenever one of us stopped, the other had to take over, with no questions asked. Length of time was not a factor, we might continue for half the lesson, or stop after just a few sentences. It was a word 'ball game', which kept us both on our toes and got promising results.

Giles worked hard for drama, so I undertook some of the more difficult forms for CSE English, getting some A level teaching as a reward. We talked, endlessly, about the best way to do things , in both subjects, and it seemed just the right time to put the ideas into print. I had just taken a book out of Cheshunt library, on Nigerian myth, and there was a fascinating tale about the making of the earth. It sounded like a good drama lesson, with every facet of human behaviour mirrored by the actions of the 'Gods'. It was to become the first story, in the text that Giles and I were to write together, 'WORLDS OF ENGLISH AND DRAMA', which was published by Oxford University Press.

Using myth and legend from all over the world, we offered concrete ideas in the running of drama sessions, suggestions for creative writing, and a great many very specific tasks in English, including grammar exercises. We were, it now seems, well ahead of our time! Every task was tried and tested, which was fun, and quite salutary, when an apparently splendid idea, just didn't work in practice. Giles' friend, Robert, a talented teacher of art, designed some absolutely wonderful illustrations, very Pre-Raphaelite and Aubrey Beardsley, and I loved them. Unfortunately, OUP had an in-house artist, and they suddenly decided to let him do five of the ten drawings, so, despite a fight, we lost half Robert's magnificent work. It made us very angry, and we resolved to find a different publisher for our next book.

Ernest was now 62, and, to his surprise, he heard that he could take early retirement, with the attractive offer of extra pay for two years. He was getting very tired of the daily haul to London, and thought, longingly, of being able to watch weekday cricket, on TV, from the comfort of his favourite armchair. He might even be able to do some more umpiring at Cuffley Cricket Club, where he was said to be remembered as responding to cries of, "Owzat, Dad?" when Paul was bowling, with a kindly, "Near enough, son!" as he quickly raised a forefinger.

He asked me what I thought, and I immediately agreed that it was a very good idea. He had an incipient duodenal ulcer, and stress, through frequent train cancellations, was bad for him. He took up the offer, and before the cricket season began, he was at home all day, ready to enjoy his new life of leisure. His daily chore was walking the dog, Freddie, and his daily delight was selecting winners of the day's races, and putting 10p win Patents and Yankees on at the local bookies, just around the corner from 'Little Gidding'.

Before he could settle, gracefully, into a lovely rut of his own choice, we had a surprise invitation to one of the many summer Royal Garden

Parties at Buckingham Palace. It is definitely thrilling to get a letter from the Queen, but we knew that there would be several hundred others there, so we didn't get carried away. I had a hat and a navy and white dress that would do, and Ernest wore one of the suits he had had made at Curly's very upmarket tailor's shop. Paul was at home, writing 'Jouer Un Role', a book of classroom plays, in French, so he agreed to drive us to the Palace.

We got there on time, joining a queue to get through the gate into the yard, where the sentries stand, The walk through the formal rooms, to get to the garden, was impressive, with thick carpet and ornate staircases. The gardens themselves are vast, and there was a roped off area, where we assumed the Queen would make her appearance. Guests were already lined up, behind the rope, to get as close as possible to the main attraction of the afternoon. We made the decision to explore the gardens, rather than stand around waiting for something to happen, so we walked down to the beautiful lake and manicured flowerbeds. We heard a ripple of applause from the guests who were standing near the palace building, and assumed that Her Majesty had arrived, but that was as near as we came to shaking the royal hand. The refreshments were in a series of open tents at one side of the main lawn, so we had a cup of tea and some Swiss roll, and I took an extra slice to give to Charlie, at school. Paul duly picked us up from the palace gates and we went out to dinner, to celebrate the occasion.

At that time, I had absolutely no thoughts of joining Ernest in retirement. Working with Giles and Charlie was like a breath of fresh air, and we had a very good set of Fifth Formers in the Drama Groups. However, one particularly annoying meeting of senior staff, changed all that, and the prospect of leaving, suddenly seemed extremely attractive. The very next morning I saw the Head and asked to be considered for early retirement. He was taken aback and appeared genuinely sorry to lose me, but, by then, I was enthusiastic about the whole thing. Hertfordshire was, at the time, offering early retirement to older teachers, as a way of reducing staffing numbers, and I had taught in the county for thirty years, so they readily agreed to my request..

We decided to let the drama groups do one final big show, so that I could leave with a bang, and Giles devised a scenario, that was reminiscent of 'The Boy Friend'. It would include absolutely everything: some music hall numbers, the Charleston, a little romance, and a rip-roaring finale. He called it 'Just For You', and it was especially meant to please Ernest, and it certainly did. All thirty of the drama group members had a part in the show. It was energetic and fun, and quite spectacular, with a colourful floral swing at the centre of the stage. They sang with gusto, and even managed to make the dancing look graceful. We all had a wonderful time.

There was to be one final event to mark my exit from Riversmead, my leaving party. Cliff had told the school secretary that he would come, wherever he was in the world. It was really sweet of him, but it made me determine to make very sure, before the date was settled, that he was going to be in England. The last thing I wanted was to upset his schedule of visits, and bring him from the other side of the world, back to Cheshunt, for my retirement do. The good news was, that he would be at home, in Weybridge, in June. A keen tennis player himself, he always went to Wimbledon, and in 1982 there was a special reason to be there, in the shapely form of Miss Sue Barker.

I did not want a formal dinner party, with speeches and testimonials from the governing body. The evening should be something we all enjoyed and I loved American line dancing. I had even had a go at teaching it in General Studies lessons, so I asked for a square dance. We had a really good evening and Sue Barker came with Cliff, even though it meant missing the Wimbledon Ball. The caller got everyone to join the dancing, and kept the action fairly simple for the non-athletic. Cliff made a very flattering farewell speech, reminding the guests that I was an inveterate enthusiast. Finally, the Head presented me with that symbol of 'time-goes-by', a clock. Midnight came, and we all went home.

Although there were several weeks left, before we broke up for the summer holidays, I felt that my stay at Riversmead had really ended. Despite occasional setbacks, I had enjoyed the past thirty years. I had taught almost everything, from Rural Science, (to Cliff's youngest sister,

Joan), French to the less able, who, by the end of the year, had learnt very little French, but knew all the words of La Marseillaise, and spells in the RE, History, and Geography departments. More importantly, I felt that I had left drama in a very strong position, under the tender, loving care and sharp eyes of Charlie and Giles. Recently, I had started meeting pupils, who would tell me that I had taught their mothers, and it was, certainly, time to go before the unwelcome news that I had taught their grandmothers. The end of term came, and to my surprise, I didn't even feel sad, as I loaded the car with all my bits and pieces, and drove back home to 'Little Gidding'.

I had not quite decided what to do next. Certainly not supply teaching, but something challenging, that might open doors to an exciting new world. For the previous ten years, I had been dabbling in the teaching of English to foreigners, EFL, and had already had several private pupils. A Japanese girl of 18, Masako, had stayed with us at 'Little Gidding' for a month, prior to going to university in Stockholm. I had taken her to school with me, and she taught my form 'Silent Night', in Japanese, which caused some surprise to their parents, when they sang it at the Carol service in December. There was also a very pleasant French boy, and I passed him on to Mike, who taught him Masefield's poem, 'Sea Fever', with "a tall ship" becoming, "a tall sheep", however hard Mike tried.

My father had taught English to private pupils, so I decided to find out how to get an EFL qualification. It turned out that there was a two year study, which one could take at evening classes, which was useless to me, as I wanted something much more immediate. Apparently, 'The Bell School', a top, if rather expensive, language school in Cambridge, offered a concentrated three month's course, leading to a recognised qualification. There was no guarantee that certification would follow, and the passing of the exam was essential, but, after thirty years teaching English to the English, I was pretty sure I could cope with that!

I rang The Bell School, and they invited me for an interview. It felt like going to Central, all over again. The journey to Cambridge took about an hour, but it was against the traffic and on the A 10, with a 70mph speed limit. The tutor I met was rather discouraging. She did not feel it would be possible to do such concentrated study, driving fifty miles each way. I should come and stay in Cambridge, at least, during the week. I told her that that was simply not an option. I had a husband and a home to look after and I would have added 'and a dog', but she didn't look like someone who could take a joke. She pointed out that there would be a lot of homework, but I just assured her that that would not be a problem.

By this time, I was beginning to wonder whether 'The Bell School' was for me, or I for them, when, suddenly, she gave a tight smile and said, "Well, if you're sure?", and I was in. The course would start in two weeks time, and when I told Ernest what the fees were, he clearly thought the whole thing was an expensive waste of time, but, as ever, he wished me luck with my new project. I can remember very little of the time in Cambridge, except that I liked the city itself, and got very used to driving there and back. The journey gave me time to get my thoughts together at the beginning of the day, and to go over what I'd learnt, and relax, on the way home.

As someone who had taught English for a long time, much of what we did, surprised me. They called it looking through binoculars the wrong way, and I certainly had not realised the problems of taking in a completely new set of sounds. Apparently, foreigners quickly learnt words that sounded the same in their own language, particularly if they were naughty words, though the meaning might be totally different in English. They illustrated this very well, when, without warning, the tutor started the lesson in some outlandish tongue, impatiently waiting for answers to questions, and giving us instructions that we didn't understand. Suddenly he stopped, and spoke in English. "That was Greek. did it sound like anything you knew? Remember, that is probably what English sounds like to a Greek!" It was a memorable moment.

Like Central, it was a small group on the course, and we got on reasonably well. One or two wanted to teach abroad and needed an accepted qualification to get a job, and they were all keen to get the exam over and start work. I seemed to be the only dilettante, and I was certainly the only one who had retired. The exam came and went, two of the group failed and had to try again, and we had a farewell party in 'The

Smuggler's Cave'. We said goodbye, and I never saw any of them again, but, at last, I had a bona fide 'English as a Foreign Language Certificate' from the College of Preceptors!

So far, nothing had upset Ernest's retirement plans, and it was only when I suggested that we move house, that it occurred to him that Cheshunt might not be our home for the rest of our lives. I suggested that Cambridge could be a good place to retire to, and he vaguely hoped that nothing would come of the idea. We went to see two or three houses, but 'Little Gidding' was still unsold , and we missed, at least, one very good bargain. Despairing of Cambridge, we looked at North Wales, where I had lots of drama friends, but it was rather dark and grey, even in the sun. Paul had taken a job at Bramcote, a boys' prep school in Scarborough, and he asked if we had considered York. No, we hadn't, but it was worth a try.

I persuaded Ernest to come up to York for a long weekend and we stayed in a hotel in the city centre. Two house viewings had been arranged, in advance, but I hadn't liked either of them, and he was very fed-up. We would never find anything, he said, because I was too difficult to please. We should stay in Cheshunt, and not move at all, and he would not come to any more houses, as he had a bad cold. Paul arrived from Scarborough for the afternoon, so leaving Ernest watching the racing on telly, we went to do yet another sweep around the estate agents.

We struck lucky at Jackson, Stops & Staff, and they told us about a house they had been given that morning. There had been no time to get a brochure together, but it was opposite the racecourse, and we could go round and see it, if we wanted to. We positively sprinted back to the car, just in case they sold the wretched house before we got there. We were prepared for failure, but 'too difficult to please' had stung me, and I was determined to prove Ernest wrong.

Mount Vale definitely looked interesting. It was made up of substantial Victorian houses, facing the racecourse, with big front gardens, so we parked round the corner and walked back to find 220. It was just what we had hoped for, double-fronted, with lovely big, bay windows, and there seemed to be a side entrance. We looked down the gap between the two houses, and there was a paved courtyard. At the back of 220, there appeared to be an attached cottage and our hearts sank, as probably it owned the courtyard, and there would be no back garden to the main house. Disappointed, we rang the front door bell and met the owner. When we mentioned that the agent had sent us, he explained that he was worried about showing us the house, before they got it tidy for visitors. Not to worry, we said, untidy will be fine, and he agreed to let us have a quick look.

It was a dream, and exactly what we had been looking for. A large kitchen, led out of a roomy breakfast room, and there was a spacious drawing room and a separate dining room. There was also a wine cellar, a downstairs cloakroom and four double bedrooms. What more could we want? The answer was a garden for Ernest. They say if it looks too good to be true, it probably is. 220, Mount Vale was just that. We completed the tour and then asked the big question. What about the cottage on the courtyard at the back, and is there a garden? When the owner said that the cottage belonged to the house, and there was a nice big garden, as well as a coach house, they had been meaning to renovate, we almost shouted for joy. Instead we asked if we could bring Ernest round the next day, and I said we would probably buy the house. They were asking for offers over £72,500, which we could afford with no difficulty.

When we got back to the hotel, Ernest was feeling slightly better, but still rather pessimistic about the likely result of our house hunting. He said he supposed we hadn't found anything. I told him that we had, and he said "Thank God!" When he saw the house the following day, he was delighted, and I was forgiven for my intransigence. Of course, we bought it.

What to call the house, was the next question. None of us could come up with anything apposite, so I phoned Giles, who promised to give the matter some thought. He rang the next day. The number was 220, opposite the racecourse where distances are in furlongs there are 220 yards in a furlong, so what about 'FURLONG HOUSE"? What a brilliant idea, and he gave us a beautiful big brass nameplate as a housewarming gift.

We had a buyer for 'Little Gidding', so we were anxious to move as soon as possible. As usual with house sales, there were blips. We lost our purchaser, but, very fortunately, there was a reserve, who snapped up the option. Nothing more could go wrong, so we watched the moving men clear the house in Cheshunt and drive away. We put 'Baby', into the cat box, loaded Freddie, the dog, into the back of the car, with some of my smaller house plants, and drove off to York.

We didn't hurry, as we had arranged for a key to be left in the courtyard, and had told the moving men where to find it. It was February and, by the time we got to the Knavesmire, the light was just beginning to fade. We were slightly surprised that the moving van had not arrived. Perhaps they'd stopped for lunch? We hoped they wouldn't be long, as it was now starting to get dark. Another half an hour later, we were seriously worried. I asked Ernest what he had said, when he gave the men the address. He looked puzzled, "I didn't give them the address. I thought you did!" It gently started to snow.

I went out into the front garden, to have one last desperate look along the road. Ernest was quietly moaning, that we would never see our furniture again, or for that matter our clothes, or our books or.... At that moment, I saw the removal van drive slowly along the road, going out of town. I rushed into the house, picked up my car keys, and went into the courtyard. Jumping into the car, I drove out onto the main road, and off in the direction I had seen the van disappear. After a minute I spotted it again, driving back in the other direction. I flashed my headlights and they saw me. They had been driving around for an hour, desperately looking for a hint as to where the house might be. Each of the men had thought the other had the address. All they knew was that the key was under a stone in the courtyard of the house, which was 'opposite the racecourse'. This was their only clue, and it was a very big racecourse, with several sides, and lots of houses with courtyards. We all thanked goodness, for a happy ending!

Chapter 14

After such an inauspicious start, it is good to record that we had made a very wise move, to a beautiful town. Best of all, were the people of Yorkshire. We met Pat, who made our lives happy, by keeping the house and the cottage in wonderful order. She had boundless energy and a great sense of humour. Then there was Steve, a bee-keeping builder, who stopped things falling down around our ears and kept us laughing. He had a really good saying, "It's the squeaky wheel that gets the oil!", to describe customers, like me, who kept trying to get him round to do a job. They were two of the nicest people you could ever meet, anywhere. We joined Ryedale Bridge Club, that met every Monday, at New Earswick. We particularly liked Shirley and Evelyn, and soon we were having them to supper, and going to supper with them. We had the beginnings of a 'network'!

Ernest set to work on the garden, quickly improving it out of all recognition. He dug out a vegetable plot, clearing away weeds, cutting dead wood from the trees, and making attractive flower beds all round the lawn. He had become an expert, and this was his third renovation. I was on a different project. The coach house, that the previous owner had 'never got round to' renovating, was a temptation I just could not resist. Despite Ernest's sensible suggestion, that I wait a bit, I had already had an architect plan the work, and get estimates for doing it, before we had even completed the buying of the house. In contemporary terms, "I don't do waiting", I never have.

One of the nice surprises about retiring from teaching was that, not only do you get a monthly injection of cash from a pension, but you also get a lump sum, to cheer you on your way. The fact that you have paid for it in contributions, over the years, is immaterial, it still seems like money for nothing! Hertfordshire gave me £14,000, which was more cash than I had ever had in my whole life, and I couldn't wait to spend it. That didn't take long, and by the time the renovation of the coach house was over, it had all gone.

As the coach house was above the car port in the courtyard, we had to plan an entry door. The surveyor suggested access from a wrought iron, spiral staircase, through the end wall by the garden, and I loved the idea. Then we added large bay windows and a smart front door, at the top of the staircase. Inside, we preserved the beamed, barn-like structure, and kept the little fireplace that had not been used for decades. It was a big space, long rather than wide, and it easily housed a bathroom and a kitchen. We added a studio couch, hanging space for clothes, a chest of drawers, a desk and lots of horse brasses, then, abracadabra, we had an attractive, fully equipped, self-contained studio, just the thing for holiday guests. The lump sum had only covered the building work, so Paul, Ernest and I did the decorating, painting the walls white and the beams black. When we had finished, it looked very attractive.

The cottage also got a new lease of life. The gas central heating was expensive, but essential, in the north of England. They had to bring gas into the cottage from the main house, and we put in a new kitchen and redecorated everything from top to bottom. A washing machine and big chest freezer went into the old 'tack room', next to the cottage, and we had window boxes made to give a rural atmosphere to the Yorkshire-stone paved courtyard. Lots of tubs with scarlet geraniums, white marguerites and blue lobelia completed the magical transformation into a holiday paradise. Over the years, it proved to be, what they call, 'a nice little earner', and, as we told the tax man about any money we took, we felt quite virtuous.

We advertised the cottage in the Sunday Telegraph holiday column and got quite a few bookings, including a retired couple asking for a discount, as they only had their pensions. One holiday agency offered to let it for us, and I thought that that was a good idea, as there seemed to be a lot of hassle, and expense, in doing it yourself. Ernest had some doubts, but we gave the firm a trial, and they did splendidly, charging much more than we would have, which more than covered their fees.

Giles and I were still writing text books together, and 'In on the Act' that covered Speech, Drama and English skills, was published by Cambridge University Press. For each activity, the springboard was a story that sounded incredible but was, actually, true. Giles did all the research and I especially liked the one about the woman who claimed to be one of the Russian royal family, who had survived the massacre after the revolution. We did one final book, with the idea of 6th formers, who weren't taking an exam, having work to do that was both interesting and challenging. Calling it 'Dead On Time', Giles wrote a very good story about terrorist activity in London, and so the idea was really up to date.

Each chapter had, at its end, things for the student to do, including such run of the mill exercises as filling in an application form, and it would have been immensely useful to hard-pressed English teachers looking for good material. The publishers liked it, but insisted on presenting it in a sort of workbook form, with the text in mock micro-film. It was, we felt, quite an inappropriate format, as like Norman, all those years ago, it was in 'all them little lines'. However, they were paying us, we hoped, so they had their way. It didn't sell well, and we got absolutely nothing for all our work. It was a waste of a very good idea.

Also, by this time, I was thinking of ways of using my Cambridge EFL qualification, and I took a look at the language schools in York. There were several, and I chose the largest, most expensive one, asking if they needed any part-time staff?. Yes, they did, so could I start on Monday? Yes, I could. They gave me a teaching group of eight young Saudi men, who were delightfully vague about what they were doing in England. My guess was having fun, at their parents' considerable expense. They certainly did not want to make any exhausting efforts to learn English. They kept telling me how tired they were, as they had gone to bed so late. I got very bored, as I couldn't really tell them off, because the school wanted to keep their tuition fees.

When I got my salary at the end of the week, I found that, after tax, I was earning less than £5 an hour, which was ridiculous. The Saudis were probably paying more than that each, and there were eight of them. I resigned, and explained that I thought it was too badly paid, to be worthwhile. They completely understood, (no doubt it had happened before), and asked if we would like to be a 'host family', which paid much better? I rang Ernest and he agreed we could give it a try. Surprisingly, it proved to be great fun, less tiring than giving EFL lessons, and reasonably profitable financially. It also worked well from the school's point of view, because we lived fairly high on the hog, in a lovely house and I couldn't resist giving the foreign guests free extra tuition, when they were with us in the evening and at weekends.

Our first guest was a charming, middle-aged Italian doctor, who was delighted to have the Coach House Studio as a base, and enjoyed learning some of the 'Ruthless Rhymes for Heartless Homes' that I taught him. He was very taken with the romantic A.E. Housman poem, 'When I was one and twenty', and, as I had always thought, verse gave him a feeling for the intonation pattern of English, that helped him considerably. Ernest organised Sunday afternoon car tours, visiting places in the beautiful countryside around York, which the guests appreciated, and he enjoyed. They would stop somewhere for afternoon tea, and Ernest would explain the mysteries of the game of cricket, which was good for their comprehension skills, in more ways than one.

Everything worked so well, that the language school kept us busy, and we had some very up-market, interesting guests. The French manager of Rowntree's chocolate in Europe, who lived in the south of France and had a private racecourse in the grounds of his house, invited us to dine with him in the summer, and we went, when we were in the area. We entertained several Norwegians and Swedes, and a few Germans, and after a bit, we could tell if the next week or so was likely to be heavy going. York Races were a sure fire attraction and I was very amused when a Swedish guest said, quite seriously, "You always lose zee money at zee races: why not throw it in zee river?" How true! Sadly, our contact with the language school was torpedoed, by what was apparently a ridiculous ruling. They let us know that, from the following month, students had to be transported to the school in the morning, and collected from it at the end of the day, two periods when the traffic congestion, in York city centre, would be at its worst. We explained the difficulty, and resigned from the host family list.

We were beginning to get into the swing of things in the north, when we heard from Cliff, that he was coming up to North Yorkshire, to do a Gospel Concert in Harrogate, and would we like to come? We were delighted to accept and invited him to come out for a meal afterwards. I knew that Cliff enjoyed Indian food, so we booked a table at Shabab's, which had very good reputation, and Paul asked two of his friends on the Bramcote staff, Richard and Philip, to join us. It was a really enjoyable evening, and the concert was a rousing success. Cliff, with Bill, who was by then his road manager, met us, afterwards, at Shabab's, where the sound of the gentle strumming of a sitar, the delicious smell of Indian cooking, and the exotic décor, gave just the right atmosphere, and by the time the delicious meal ended, my five companions were happily chatting away.

I wanted to avoid any awkwardness, about who should pay, so, I caught the waiter's eye, and gave him, what I thought was my credit card, asking him to use it to settle the bill. Cliff and Bill were keeping us entertained, with stories of happenings on the tour, when the waiter returned. Very politely, in his musical Indian voice, he said, "I am very sorry, madam, but we do not accept North Yorkshire Library cards!" I still think that this was number one, the top of my embarrassing moments.

I had never actually tried supply teaching in a comprehensive school, and maybe, my feeling that it would be unsatisfactory from everyone's point of view, was wrong, so I phoned the local education office and put my name on the supply list. It seemed to be surprisingly well-paid, and I was interested in making contact with other teachers of English. Almost immediately, the office rang back, offering me an afternoon's work for the following week. Nearly all the school staff would be out on an in-service training course, discussing the problems that had arisen through the amalgamation of two comprehensives, and I agreed to report at 1.30p.m., on Monday, to help to hold the fort. It turned out to be an ominously good analogy. When I arrived, things appeared to be slightly chaotic, as several supply teachers were involved, but, work had been set, and so it was merely supervision that was needed. The deputy head pointed at a door in the main corridor, and said that that was to be my base, and classes would report to me, for their lessons. They were all fourth years, the subject was always English, and with work set, it should be easy; money for jam.

I opened the door of the classroom and all hell was raging inside. Books were being thrown about, and a minor war was being raged, over who should sit where. There was a brief pause in hostilities, when they saw a stranger enter, followed by, "Where's our proper teacher? Who are you?". They barely waited for an answer, before their private wars restarted. It looked an impossible battle, but I had taught too long to be intimidated by fifteen-year-olds. I shouted them into some kind of order, and tried to get them started on the work that had been set. Whatever that was, they didn't know, they hadn't got the text books and the teacher had got their English exercise books, so, even if they had a pen, which they hadn't, they couldn't do it, even if they knew what it was, which they didn't.

It was like some awful comedy farce, in which I had been given a ghastly leading role. Every time the bell went there was a change of cast, but the unruly scenario always seemed to be the same. I felt really sorry for their teachers, who must be very glad to be out of the school, for a whole afternoon of peace and quiet. The school day was to end at four and, by the last lesson, I was really angry. What a total waste of everyone's time. I let chaos reign for the final lesson, and wrote a verse, based entirely on what was happening, at that particular moment. I thought that it was important that they recognise the time they had wasted and the resulting hell that they had created, so all the quotes in the verse were exactly what they had said. By a terrible irony, I had found out that the comprehension questions they were supposed to be doing, were based on "All Quiet on the Western Front"!

At a quarter to four, I took my shoe off and banged the heel on the desk. They were surprised enough to be, briefly, totally silent. I spoke to them coldly and told them, in words of one syllable what, as an adult, I thought of their behaviour, that they had bored me out of my mind, and I felt really sorry for the teachers who had to deal with them every day. They were surprised. They had expected a shouting match. I told them about the verse and suggested that, if they listened carefully, they might recognise some of the things they had said. Then I read them my 'Ode to Mrs Unsworth', their teacher.

ODE TO MRS UNSWORTH A Fraternal Lament

An afternoon at this school
With the Fourths, is quite a wow!
There's lots of things they ought to do,
And books to tell them how.
Some English Comprehension work,
(Ten questions at the rear),
'All Quiet on the Western Front'?
Well, they're not quiet here!

The buzz of busy chat goes round
The room. There's little done,
Except to lose a pen or two.
"Miss, can you lend me one?"
"He's chucking things!"
"She tripped me up!"
"The disco's on today...."
The yammering of so many tongues,
The non-stop, "Here, I say!"

One afternoon of wasted time,
Another day gone wrong,
It's such a pity they don't know
Youth's here.....
And then it's gone.

They were genuinely impressed that anyone could write anything in the noisy chaos of a lesson. "Did you really just make that up?" they asked. I assured them that I had. Then the bell went, and they left quietly, some of them congratulating me on the verse as they passed my desk. As soon as I got home I phoned the education office and resigned from future supply work. I wrote out a copy of the verse for their teacher and posted it to her, with an explanatory note. She did not reply.

I had done some examining of Drama at O level, in the south, before we moved to York, and when I was asked to continue in the north of England, I was pleased to say that I would. It was a good decision and, very soon I knew schools, like the modern comprehensive in Wath-upon-Dearn, where William Hague had been a pupil, and Christ's Hospital in Lincoln, where the old building and traditions, made it seem a world away from the new concept of a secondary school. Sometimes Ernest came with me and we stayed in a B & B, so that, when I had finished the examining, we could go sight-seeing. I got to stay in some very different towns, like Hull and Blackburn, and Scunthorpe and Bolton, and it was cheering to see what very good work was getting done, and how hard many young drama teachers were working.

Once, in Durham, when I was on my own, I decided to stay the night, as the examining would take two days. I hadn't booked anywhere, but there are a lot of guest houses in this popular tourist town. Picking a pleasant looking house, with a 'Vacancy' sign, I rang the bell. The woman, who came to the door, gave a cry of recognition. "I know you, don't I?". I felt like Charles Causley must have, as I had never seen her before in my life. I told her that she was mistaken, but she simply wouldn't believe me. She was so sure that we knew each other, that I began to wonder if we really did. Then she gave a gasp of embarrassment, "I'm so sorry, I've just realised, it's because I saw you on that TV programme last night, about Cliff Richard. That's why I thought I knew you!" So the mystery was solved. I had been interviewed by Gloria Hunniford, and someone had seen my brief moment of fame.

I was even sent up to Edinburgh, with both Ernest and Paul coming for the ride, and, after breakfast, they went off to a race meeting at Hamilton. I had a busy morning, and in the afternoon, the school hall was very warm and stuffy. The school dinner had been rather filling, but the chips were delicious. The house lights went down as the first group began their play, and the next thing I knew was the lights came up at the end. I had fallen asleep. Luckily, I didn't think anyone had noticed, as their attention had been focused on the stage, and I had woken up just in time. It made the discussion part of the exam extremely useful. I asked all about their 'motivation', and how they felt their play had gone. By the time the questioning had ended, I felt I'd seen the performance, but I kept my marks on the generous side. When I thought about it afterwards, the whole horror of the potential disaster made my blood run cold. I could almost see the headlines, "EXAMINER FALLS ASLEEP AS STUDENTS ACT", and I resolved never to let it happen again, and it never did.

Chapter 15

We had arrived in York in 1984, which happened to be one of the years for the outdoor performance of the Mystery Plays, dating from the Middle Ages. We managed to get seats in the park, and took a rug and some cushions with us, in case the chairs were hard and we got cold. The play told the story of the crucifixion , and the cast were all amateurs, except for Jesus, himself. It was tremendously well done, and totally believable, except that some of the crowd on Calvary, wore white track shoes, which looked odd, with their Roman tunics. The cross was huge, and I was quite worried when Jesus was fixed to it with leather thongs, so it was a relief to see that there was a partially hidden footrest, to stop him slipping off. We had a very interesting evening.

At 'The English Martyrs' church, the next morning, the priest taking the ten-thirty mass, looked faintly familiar. I whispered to Ernest that I was sure he'd been in the play. Afterwards, we met him at the church doorway, and he told us he was playing one of the Sanhedrin, and thoroughly enjoyed acting. We asked him to come for coffee when he was free, so that we could chat about drama, and that's how we came to know Father Hugh. He was a wonderful parish priest and an exceptionally talented impressionist, who did a superb imitation of Liberace, piano playing and all, for the Irish priests' show. He was a delightful man, and he became a real brick in my wall of friendship.

Staff and parents at Bramcote, in Scarborough, also turned out to be great social contacts. It was good to meet teachers, like Richard, who worked his socks off as head of English, and organised a huge number of extra-curricular activities, like theatre visits and quizzes, and camping and canoeing and orienteering, and so on, which must have taken up all his waking hours. I just hoped that everyone appreciated his efforts. There were some very interesting parents, and we came to know a few of them quite well, as Paul got more and more involved with out of school activities. It was an eye opener for me to see how good the parent/staff relationships were at Bramcote, compared with the disappointing lack of trust we had found in some of the mums and dads at Riversmead. Perhaps there are some people who do not appreciate things they get for nothing?

York was a town that all our friends seemed to like. It had so many interesting places to visit, and there was wonderful countryside, within easy driving distance, like the dales and the Yorkshire moors. Janice and Mike came, and Sue and Jim, and even Cliff, when he was touring a show in the north. Nigel, who had been my favourite at Broxbourne Bridge Club, and was now our solicitor, visited with his attractive new wife, Nicky. They brought a really interesting present, the beautifully framed, hand-written, earliest deeds of 'Furlong House', which turned out to have been originally owned by a 'cow keeper'. We hung it in the new Coach House Studio, where future guests often had a try at reading the obscure legal phrasing, written by lawyers who were paid by the number of words, so the longer the better.

A knock on the front door one day, revealed a man who asked if we wanted to have the house painted. Ernest pointed out that we had just spent over a thousand pounds having it redecorated, but it seemed that the offer was to paint a picture for us. When he told us that it would only cost about ninety pounds, we thought it was worth a try. He sat, opposite the house, on the Knavesmire and, two days later, brought us the result of his efforts. It was very good and we bought it. Apparently, he rode on his bike from town to town, camping overnight, and when he saw an interesting house, he would offer to do a picture. He said it was a great way to live, and that, so far, no one had turned down the finished article.

The artist was very taken with a leaded glass panel, over the front door, which Ernest had chosen when a representative from a local art and craft studio, called. She carried a book of illustrations, and Ernest loved a design, showing a couple doing the Charleston, all 1920s and full of life. We went to see the studio to pay, and I was fascinated by the techniques of glass cutting and lead soldering. The firm was run by two women, who said they had learnt all they knew at an evening class, so I was keen to follow in their footsteps. I phoned the further education college and found that there was a leaded-glass course starting in a fortnight, so I enrolled, there and then.

Two of the Bramcote parents we had got to know quite well, were Mary and Bob, who lived in a fascinating house in Boston Spa, where the hunt had once gathered. The huge Victoria plum tree in their garden, had provided the main ingredient for my jam-making, for the past two years, and I really liked them. I gave Mary a ring to tell her about the course, and to my delight she said she would join as well. We had a ball. The tutor was a woman, who was truly expert, and very likeable. She dealt calmly with all the disasters that came with such a very accident-prone material as glass, giving us the necessary confidence to press the cutter down really hard, when we were worried the glass would crack along the wrong line. We learnt to stretch, cut and solder the lead, without damaging ourselves. Mary, who was artistic, made a fascinating design for a door, and I managed to make a simple panel of diamond shapes, in coloured glass, to go in the kitchen. At 'Furlong House', leaded glass ruled OK, and we later had various pictures of horses, made for the coach house.

We tried a car rally for our York friends, but the distances between villages seemed too long for a comfortable evening's drive, let alone answer clues on the way, and we missed the enthusiasm of the Cheshunt gang. Holidays were, as always, important to us. Deauville, for the August race meeting, and tours in rural France were often top of our list of places to go to, but we couldn't resist a bargain cruise on a Polish ship, the 'Stefan Batori', where they called the bingo numbers in Polish. Ernest's favourite was one that sounded like 'chedjeshki-yedjindj', but we never found out what it meant, and, needless to say, we didn't win at bingo, either.

In 1986, Cliff starred, in a new musical, 'TIME', and had the wonderful experience of being a very successful actor, in a long West End run. Paul, Giles and I went with a friend, and met him for supper after the show, and he told us how much he was enjoying working in the theatre. I really loved the energy, effort and commitment that he put into everything he did, and 'Time' was hugely innovative technically, with a space ship landing on the stage, and the hologram of Laurence Olivier hovering overhead. Cliff was now reaping the rewards of his huge success, and if he wanted anything, he could, on the whole, afford it. I was absolutely delighted for him, and very moved when he later asked if we would like to stay in Tala Mai, the villa he had bought near Albufeira in the Algarve. It was the Christmas of 'Mistletoe and Wine', and I never hear the song without remembering the lovely setting of Tala Mai, near the edge of cliffs overlooking the Mediterranean. It had a glorious garden, a tennis court and a huge pool, everything one could possibly wish for, and we were tremendously impressed. We felt we were living in the lap of luxury, as we relaxed in huge armchairs, sipping our glasses of Portuguese wine. Ernest, Paul and Giles came, and Suzie, who had been a drama student at Central, and went on to run the youth activities at the National Theatre. It goes without saying that we ate well as Paul was head chef. We played 'O Hell', the card game our footballers had taught us, and we kept saying, to the empty air, 'Thank you, Cliff!'.

Paul was really enjoying teaching French at Bramcote, and was able to help Richard by driving the bus, for the school's canoeing adventures. It sounded good fun, as the party would camp in a field by a river, and cook supper over a fire. He sang in the choir, learnt the tuba to fill a space in the band, and made friends with great colleagues like John and Mary, and Penny and Diana, and the school secretary, Delia. It was just the right job. He, briefly, took violin lessons, till, when he sat his grade 3 test, the examiner suggested that he might, perhaps, like to try some other instrument!

We had settled down, happily in York. James had married the delightful Karen in 1985, and their three little girls, Elizabeth, Alexandra and Georgina, had arrived in just over four years. They lived in Southgate, so we didn't see a great deal of them, but, when they did make the long journey north, we were always amazed at how much the children had grown. We put a Wendy house in our garden for them to play in, and I had a wonderful time at summer car boot sales on the Knavesmire, buying big teddies, knitted dollies and children's books.

When they moved to a new home in Southgate, we bought them a Wendy house of their own. Elizabeth, who had just learnt to write, put a notice on the door that read, "THIS HOUSE BELONGS TO THE NORRIS GRILS", and 'The Grils' they were, from then on. Karen was very fond of horses, so we managed to find a riding school, just outside York, where they all had lessons. Riding became a 'must', when they came to stay.

At the time, I was really interested in making decorative arrangements of dried flowers, and managed to get an account with a wholesaler in Leeds. I had also taken over a nearby allotment in 1985, ostensibly to grow asparagus, but flowers, that could be easily dried, seemed a much better bet. I had so many, that I sold quite a few bunches from our front garden at Furlong House. I had my usual optimistic hopes of creating a world-wide production of flower trees, with Karen. I made a start by selling dried flower arrangements, to the staff at the Terry's chocolate factory, beside the racecourse, but, as ever, something else caught my attention, and that was the end of that particular enthusiasm.

Our invitation to stay in Cliff's glorious villa in the Algarve, had been very generously repeated each year since 'Mistletoe and Wine', but by 1988, we usually went in the autumn, at half-term. There were eight of us, Giles, Jan and Mike, Richard, the three of us, and Michael, from North Wales. Everyone was tremendously grateful, as late October was exactly the point at which exhausted teachers needed a break. Paul came up with the splendid idea that it might be fun to give the holiday a literary flavour, by reading the novels short-listed for The Booker Prize, and then, taking a vote on which, in our opinion, should win. We would see if the official verdict was the same as ours. We agreed that each of us would buy one of the books, read it and then, in Portugal, pass it on to the others. We all would have the whole week to get through the other five, albeit rather sketchily. Some would be easier to promote than others, so we would draw lots to decide who should introduce which book.

It all went according to plan. The selection, by the official committee, on the whole, met with our approval, and it was great to read novels, by contemporary authors, that we would probably never have found time for in our busy teaching lives. There was, however, one book that none of us cared for: 'The Famished Road', by Ben Okri, a young Nigerian. It seemed a strange selection for the best novel of the year, as it was immensely difficult to get into. The techniques of so-called 'magical realism', effectively disguised any narrative line, and none of us could say, with confidence, what it was about. We were all quite certain of one thing, however. It definitely would not win the the Booker Prize.

As the Chairman of our unofficial committee, Paul had organised the drawing of lots, to decide who should present which book. He passed the hat round, and we each drew a carefully folded piece of paper. I opened mine, to find the one name I had dreaded; 'The Famished Road'. I let out a groan of despair, and then, surprisingly, groans came from all round the table, for Paul had played a trick on us, and all the slips of paper bore the same title. He was hugely amused. We were all greatly relieved, and had a good laugh when, in the real drawing of lots, Paul, himself, drew 'The Famished Road'. Later, to everyone's total amazement, we heard that Ben Okri, anagrammed by us into 'Ink Bore', had won the Booker.

For some reason, while I was teaching, I had taken out an endowment policy that cost ten pounds a month. Now in 1989, it matured, and it seemed like money for nothing. The lump sum I got when I retired, had disappeared on worthwhile projects, and I was determined that this windfall should be used for fun. But doing what? Ernest's cautious reaction was predictable. He thought we should save it; one never knew what might happen, but whatever I decided was fine with him. Paul's reaction was also predictable. Let's spend it; one never knew what might happen, but whatever I decided was fine with him. I'd always wanted to go round the world, so that's what the three of us did.

When I suggested it, Ernest was delighted. Cricket test matches had made the southern hemisphere attractive, and names like Melbourne and Sydney rang with the sounds of leather on willow that he loved. The one possible snag was that we would be spending long hours in the air, and he had had a minor heart attack in Deauville, two years previously. It had been totally unexpected. He had collapsed at the entrance to the course, and been taken into the lady jockeys' changing room, to be examined by the racecourse doctor. They called an ambulance, and he was carried, on a stretcher, through the race course crowds, to the Heart Clinic in Trouville. To cheer him up, we teased him later about being the only man to have seen the lady jockeys changing. He stayed at the clinic overnight and they diagnosed possible angina, needing further investigation when we got back to England, and, meantime, he should stop smoking at once.

Ernest dealt with the whole affair wonderfully well, and his chief regret seemed to be that he had just bought a large supply of small cigars to take home. A visit to a private heart specialist in York, confirmed angina and nothing more serious, and he was given pills to take, when necessary. When asked about the proposed trip, in 1989, our doctor thought it should not be a problem, and it would be good for Ernest to have some fun. Paul had the Christmas school holidays to come, and offered to be our tour leader and organise the whole adventure. It was to be 'Round the world in twenty-six days', and so it was.

Chapter 16

We flew from Manchester to Dubai, changed planes, and then on to Hong Kong for three nights. It was before the colony was returned to China, and people were a little anxious about the looming 1997 transfer of sovereignty. Paul had some friends living there, and we were taken to dinner in an exciting tower that slowly revolved as we ate, giving us magnificent views over the city. We went to the crowded markets, saw the temples and did everything by the book. It was a real experience of another world, and a great place to shop. I bought Ernest a black kimono, embroidered with a scarlet and gold dragon, which I don't think he ever wore.

Our next stop was Melbourne, and, as it was 24th December, we hoped to have an Aussie-style Christmas dinner the next day. We were booked into a 'Flag' hotel, just outside the city for three days, so we collected the car that we were taking all the way to Sydney, and drove into town. Everywhere seemed deserted, and it turned out that the trams were on strike, so people were staying at home. However, we finally found a restaurant, had lunch and went to explore the city. The Melbourne Cricket Ground looked empty, but for Ernest and Paul, it was an icon from the past. I found the old jail much more exciting, with rows of death masks, including Ned Kelly's, and spine-chilling sounds of old Melbourne, echoing through the prison cells.

The next day we went to the zoo, and saw wallabies, and kangaroos, and a cute little koala bear. For the record, other than road-kills, these were the only animals we saw on our long overland journey to Sydney, so much for the fauna. The flora was flourishing, and the eucalyptus trees looked as though they could cope with as many climate changes as you cared to throw at them, the temperature varying from the low 90's on December 25th, to the high 50's on Boxing Day. One last impression of Melbourne was the bay where the prison ships had landed their pathetic cargo of convicts. Somehow, I felt the horror of that terrible journey was still in the air.

Any long drive is in danger, at times, of becoming slightly tedious, and a very long drive in Australia is no exception. The small towns we passed through, first in Victoria and then in New South Wales, were like the United States in the fifties: little isolated communities, cut off from the rest of humanity, for whom television must have come as a wonderful window on the outside world. We toured the old gold mines, tasted wine in the vineyards, saw lots of Aussie flags, and generally took in the ambience of the outback. We decided we did not want to move there, even though there seemed to be a pleasing lack of modern pseudo-sophistication.

Canberra turned out to be just about as exciting as any new town in England. There are parks, and lakes, and lots of very impressive public buildings, all given over to government use. The capital of Australia did not seem to have a great deal to do with real life. This impression was reinforced when, after breakfasting in an empty café, by an empty public car park, we found a parking ticket on the windscreen of our hired car. Apparently, we were going to be fined as we had done something wrong. We never tried to find out what!

The Blue Mountains were impressive, but the real gem was Sydney, and here, we did feel, was a place we could happily move to. The sweep of the glorious bay, the splendour of the harbour bridge and the familiar nautical outline of the opera house, gave the city a perceptible buzz that we had not felt since we left the crowded streets of Hong Kong. We did everything our three days allowed. We went to the races at Randwick, ate a delicious dinner on a harbour cruise, watching darkness fall and the lights come on in the houses around the bay, and paddled our feet in the warm waters of the Pacific Ocean at Bondi beach. Driving into the city, from our hotel, Paul spotted a notice warning drivers that they might be breathalysed, in a random testing programme. As he was, at that moment, in a state of total abstinence, he said it would be great fun to have the experience of blowing into the little machine, secure in the knowledge of a negative result. No sooner were the words out of his mouth, when we were flagged down and he got his wish. Fortunately, on our way back, after a good dinner and several glasses of exceptionally delicious local wine, he escaped detection.

We flew to New Zealand on New Year's Eve, arriving in time to see 1990 celebrations in Auckland. It was Ernest's birthday, and the hotel was providing entertainment by, to our dismay, an unknown British pop group. However, we decided to join in the fun, and took a seat at a table in the bar. We were not overjoyed to be asked to pay an extra fee for the privilege. We explained that we were guests in the hotel, but it seemed that made no difference, so we took a bottle of Aussie champagne up to our room, and saw the new decade in there.

Auckland appeared to be a very busy centre for leisure sailing, with innumerable little boats, darting around in a brisk wind. We drove down the North Island to Rotaroa, to see the geysers, and marvel at the tropical plants that grew everywhere. We had expected New Zealand to be like England. Another plane, to Christchurch, took us to the Canterbury plains, with huge flocks of sheep nibbling busily away at green, rather damp, grass. We were quite relieved to find that the South Island clearly had a very British climate. We had picked up our hire car, and drove towards Queenstown, to spend a night, en route, at Orari Gorge, with Rosa and Graham Peacock. The long arm of Bramcote reached as far the Antipodes, for Paul had met the family when their son was at the school. They had two homes, one in North Yorkshire, where they were experts in the breeding and artificial insemination of pedigree cattle, while the other was in New Zealand, where they owned a huge sheep station.

Orari Gorge was in the heart of the country, but we got there safely, to a wonderful welcome. The beautiful house had been built for the first Bishop of Christchurch in the nineteenth century, on land that had to be cleared of the original forest. In the garden, a bridge crossed a fast flowing little stream, which, we were told, flooded in the rainy season. I asked about the winter, and they said it seemed long, without the excitement of the Christmas break that we get in the northern hemisphere.

December was sheep shearing time and the station buzzed with activity, as the shearers went around the country in gangs, speedily moving from one farm to the next. Quite a few of the workers were very strong-looking women, and, as Ernest noted, you wouldn't pick a quarrel with any of them! The sheep submitted quietly to the indignity of being forcibly turned on their backs, grasped in a grip of iron, and having their fleece chopped off with vicious looking electric shears, then they just got back on their feet, gave a quick shake and scurried off to the nearest field to restart munching. After touring the huge sheep station in Graham's car, we had a delicious supper of roast mutton, which has much more flavour than lamb, but is never for sale in the shops. We drove off in the morning, thanking the family for their very generous hospitality, and heading for the lake at Queenstown.

Before we left home we had tried to bone up on places we knew nothing about, so that, when we got there, we could use our time well. I had not included New Zealand in my research, because I thought I knew all about it: sheep, green fields, and more sheep. I was wrong. Admittedly, there are a lot of sheep, but the North Island is subtropical, and the South Island has glorious fiords, and mountains with rushing rivers, and not too long ago, GOLD. It was discovered in 1862, by two shepherds, driving a flock to new pastures. They had to cross the Shotover River, at a ford near Queenstown, and one of them noticed a lump of sparkling stone, which turned out to be a huge gold nugget. They became instant millionaires, and retired, at once, from the shepherding business, as winners of an unlikely lottery.

The resulting rush saw the biggest finds of gold in the history of prospecting. The Shotover was named as the richest river in the entire world, and, shamefully, I'd never even heard of it. Most of the gold has gone, but they still find the occasional small nugget, and optimistic amateur prospectors keep looking. The old workings are above the river, and we took a guided minibus tour, to see them. It turned out to be hair-raising.

The track to the old gold mine ran along the side of the river canyon, and had been cut into the face of the cliff by Chinese navvies, so that the miners could get to work. It was just slightly wider than our little bus, and the edge of the cliff fell away, down to the river in a sheer drop. Paul could not bear to look out of the window, but I saw that there were no trees to break our fall, if we swerved off the road. We got safely to the old workings and noticed the cemetery, with a great many graves, as we toured the panning area. We had a go with a bucketful of sludge, and only Ernest got a glimpse of precious metal in the form of a tiny, glistening speck. There was a high bridge over the river, with a drop of about two hundred feet down to the stream, and people were doing bungee-jumps from the parapet. It looked sheer madness, and quite an expensive way of frightening yourself to death. The organisers assured me that bungee-jumping was very popular, and even old ladies had taken part. I said I thought that old ladies would have had more sense, unless they were tired of life and were looking for a dramatic way out. We decided not to have a go ourselves.

The prospect of the journey back to Queenstown had not worried us, for we assumed that the return track would be wider. To our horror, we went back exactly the same way, but, luckily, didn't meet anything coming in the opposite direction. Without question, New Zealanders do like extreme sports. They go rafting on the Shotover where the water dashes over the rapids in a whirlpool of conflicting currents, they leap off high bridges, they freefall over mountains, and seem to seek the dangers that sheep farming does not offer. No wonder they enjoy a good game of rugby, especially against the Aussies.

We went to look at a little town called Arrow, where there were some of the ramshackle buildings that had once housed immigrant families. I wanted to see inside one, but Ernest and Paul opted out, so I went alone. There was a slightly bent, grey-haired woman, already there when I arrived. When she realised that I was English, she told me that it was exactly like the shack she had lived in when she came to New Zealand, from England, after the war. Newly married, they had gone on the £10 single voyage, looking for a new life. She still had a Geordie accent, and I was fascinated to know if she had ever regretted leaving her home. My question , "If you had your time over again, would you still have come ?", brought an immediate, "No, I definitely wouldn't, but it's too late now!" Looking round the desolate shack, with no bathroom and the privy at the bottom of the garden, I could see why.

We went back via Hawaii, to Los Angeles, where we visited Disneyland and the Universal film studios, then on the twelve hour flight to Manchester. After taking us to York, Paul drove straight on to Scarborough, as the twenty-six days were over, and he had to teach the next day. He had dreadful jetlag for some time, and still insists that he taught on autopilot for weeks. But it was worth it, and Ernest suffered no apparent ill effects. To have gone right round the world was a real thrill, and we all felt the endowment had been well spent.

Our brief stay in Los Angeles, had reminded me of the delights of the East Coast, and in 1992, I persuaded Ernest to fly to Florida, and we would drive up Route 1, through Georgia and the Carolinas, to Washington and, finally, end up in New York. There would be lots to see. Paul was working, so I asked Michael, if he would come. Happily, he agreed, saying that it was a journey he had always wanted to make. We booked a flight to Orlando, and a hire car that could be handed back in New York, and we were all set. An interesting American advertisement on TV, had shown President Ronald Reagan giving British tourists a personal invitation to come to the USA. It seemed too good an opportunity to miss, so I wrote to him, saying that we were pleased to accept, and would arrive in March. Not surprisingly, we still had not had a reply by the time we left for the visit, but I resolved to ring him when we got to Washington. After all, he had invited us!

We got to Florida without any problem, went to see the rocket launching site at Cape Canaveral and enjoyed the rides at Disney World. We drove north, with Michael at the wheel, to Georgia, staying in motels en route, and eating in diners, where the food is nearly always good. Ernest tried 'grits', a rather tasteless alternative to rice, and Michael got very good at driving on American roads, in a car with a cruise control, and at carrying all our heavy cases, which was a tremendous relief. The Carolinas were really interesting, which was a good thing, as the weather was, at times absolutely appalling with the tail end of the hurricane season giving winds and lashing rain. The coastal resort motels were often closed, but we always managed to find somewhere to stay. In towns, like Charleston, we walked along streets lined with elegant eighteenth century, ante-bellum houses, then on to Jamestown, the first English settlement, and it was sad to read how many of the pioneers had died in the attempt to build a new life. Williamsburg, on the way to Washington, was very much a tourist attraction, with residents, in costume, living out the legends of long ago. Echoes of the War of Independence, and the Civil War, were everywhere; a reminder that 'freedoms' were never bought cheaply, in terms of human lives.

We finally got to Washington and decided, for a change, to stay in one of the big hotels. I was determined to try calling the White House, to let the President know that we had arrived, though both Michael and Ernest thought it was a lost cause. To my surprise, I found a number for the White House in the phone book, though it was given as the 'Tourist Office', so I rang them. A very nice girl listened, patiently, to the sad story of my letter, from England, to Ronald Reagan, and was deeply apologetic that I had not had a reply. She was sorry to tell me that he was out of town at the moment, so we would not be able to see him, however, if I would hold on, she would see what could be done to lessen my disappointment.

A minute later, a new voice came on the line, she introduced herself as 'Boots', and she apologised, yet again, on behalf of the President, but would we like a tour of The White House, the following morning? If we came early, at seven, we could be taken round by the FBI, but, if we would prefer something later, we could go around with the general public. Thanking her for her kindness, I opted for a later time, and she asked us to meet her at 'the sentry box', at ten. I should just give my name and ask for Boots. Ernest and Michael were totally amazed, and congratulated me on the success of my venture. So, the following morning, we duly took a taxi to the tourist entrance, and asked for 'Boots'. She turned out to be an attractive brunette of about 35, and immediately ushered us to the head of the long line of people, waiting to do the tour. We were introduced to the guide, and given a little American flag as a memento.

As we looked at the Oval Office, and the wonderfully elegant rooms that are used for receptions, we almost felt like important guests.

Our final stop was New York City, where I had spent such an interesting time, years before, when I had worked as a saleswoman for General Diaper Service. As well as general sight-seeing, I was keen to show Ernest the home of the editor of Fortune Magazine, on East 84th Street, where I had lived. I was quite upset when we got there, to discover that the old brownstone house had been pulled down, and a block of flats had taken its place. All too soon, our time in the USA ended, and we flew back to Manchester.

Chapter 17

We had been back in York for several weeks, before I realised that Ernest was not at all well. He got out of breath when we were out walking, and I remembered that we had often taken taxis on our American tour, because he was tired. When I suggested he should go to the doctor for a check-up, he got quite upset, so I didn't press the point. It was the last week in May, and he worked in the garden, lifting the daffodil bulbs, and pruning the fruit bushes, ready for the summer. We played bridge, as usual, on the Monday evening, but at the end of the week, when I woke up on Saturday morning, there was a strange chemical smell in the room, which came from the angina capsules, designed to relieve distress, in a heart attack related episode.

Despite Ernest's protests that he was perfectly all right, I phoned the doctor. A locum came almost immediately, and diagnosed an attack of angina, but, as a precaution, wanted him to go to York General Hospital for tests. She called an ambulance, and, though he insisted that he could walk, Ernest was carried down the stairs on a stretcher. I left a message for Paul at Bramcote to tell him what was happening, got in my car and drove to the hospital. When I got to the ward, the sister came to speak to me. They were about to do some tests, as it was not clear what was wrong, and then the doctor joined us. He, too, was very vague about how seriously ill Ernest was, but when I asked if I should call my two sons, he felt that that might be a little premature.

I went home, took Rosie, the dog, for a walk, welcomed the holiday visitors into Furlong Cottage, and then hurried back to the hospital. Ernest was in a single room, connected to various throbbing and flashing machines. He looked much better, and a cheerful staff nurse was looking after him. I was tremendously relieved. The next day, Sunday, I tried to do some work in the garden, as hospital visiting time was not until 4 o'clock, and I bought some delicious black cherries to take with me. When I got to the ward, the single room door was open, and the bed empty. My heart stopped. I quickly asked a passing nurse, where Mr Norris was, and a voice from behind another door, answered, "Try in here!", and there, in a small four-bedded ward, was Ernest. He was cheerful, and very positive about what had been confirmed as, a minor coronary. There would be certain procedures, one of which involved watching a video about how to deal with the aftermath of an attack. The patient was asked to 'bring a partner', would I come? I laughed, and said it sounded like an invitation to a thé dansant, and I was delighted to accept. As always, Ernest wondered if I was looking after myself. Had I had some lunch? Of course, I hadn't. He gave me a list of things to bring with me the next day, and, laughingly, insisted that I went back home and had a proper evening meal. He looked so well, that I agreed to do as I was told. I kissed him and left, and that was the last time I ever saw him.

At 5 o'clock in the morning, the sound of hammering on the front door, woke me. The hospital had tried to phone, but no one had answered. It was devastating news, Ernest had died, in the night, of a second heart attack. I phoned Paul and James, but I just couldn't believe what had happened, that I had lost my sweetheart, my partner and my closest friend. Nothing could ever be the same again. The next few days went by in a blur of tears. When someone dies there are so many things to be done, people to be told, certificates to be collected, a funeral to be arranged, letters to be written, but there was just one awful reality, Ernest was dead.

Family and friends came quickly to my aid. Paul and James set aside their own grief at losing their father, and dealt with spreading the terrible news, and the arrangements with the hospital and the crematorium. Father Hugh suggested that, rather than a requiem mass, we have a service with music and poetry, and Michael hurried from North Wales to help in any way he could. Pat came, with flowers, to get the house ready for visitors, and sad letters arrived by every post, for Ernest had been truly loved and appreciated.

The service at the English Martyrs church was wonderful. I had chosen extracts from 'Little Gidding', and Father Hugh had recorded them with background music. "What we call the beginning is often the end/ And to make an end is to make a beginning,/ The end is where we start from." ... "And all shall be well and/ All manner of thing shall be well..." Ernest would have loved it. We sang 'Fight the good fight' and 'He who would valiant be', to remind us of happy days with little Noddy, and Father Hugh read the prayers for the dead, in his lovely Irish voice. He had got to know Ernest very well, and when he spoke about him in a short address, he was speaking about a friend. He knew that during the war, Ernest had been in Burma, in the Intelligence Corps, but we had never discussed what rank he had held in the Army. He had, in fact, been a sergeant, but Father Hugh mistakenly referred to him as a 'Captain', and we all felt that Ernest would have been very amused, to have been given such an unexpected promotion.

The church was nearly full, but the simple pine coffin, with the spray of white lilies, looked strangely isolated on the trestles, right in front of the altar steps. Giles and Karen came from London, and Derek travelled from Flintshire. All our York friends were there, including Shirley and Evelyn from the Bridge Club, our next door neighbours, Christine, and Big Barbara and John, and new friends, like Mary, plus Richard and Delia from Bramcote. Pat and Steve came, and Steve voted it the best funeral he had ever been to.

The crematorium at Bishopthorpe, in early June, was surrounded by blossoming fruit trees, with the many flowers and wreaths from our family and friends, laid end to end on the grass, in a pathway of soft colours. We had chosen Ernest's favourite Gershwin tune, 'Rhapsody in Blue', for the last piece of music, and I shall never forget the sadness of those opening bars. Father Hugh read the final commitment, and the coffin slid out of sight, the curtains closing behind it. "The end is where we start from....."

I had wondered whether 'Furlong House', without Ernest, would be unbearable, so I was really pleased when all the memories it evoked, were happy ones. We had had such a great time, that I put away all thoughts of moving away from York. I couldn't bear to go back to the Ryedale bridge club yet, so I partnered Shirley at the York club, where I didn't know anyone. Finally, I did go back to Ryedale and had a super partner in Eva, and we got to understand each other's bids reasonably well, which is better than 'par for the course' in bridge. Paul planned a getaway tour to help me through the 1992 summer holidays, and we flew to New England. Our friends, Lizzie and John, recommended a delightful place to stay, where a judge's widow ran a comfortable guest house, in Cambridge, just outside Boston. We visited the glass museum at Harvard, and were amazed at the things they made. I did the tourist tram ride, where I learnt all about the university, and found, to my surprise, that the words, 'The Ivy League', had nothing to do with ancient walls covered in climbing plants. Originally, the results of university games were given as those in the fourth, or in Roman numerals, IV, league, and the name came from there. We watched whales, visited the witch town of Salem and dined on delicious Maine lobsters. We toasted our 'absent friend' everywhere we went, but it was vital that I accepted the awful truth, that Ernest really had gone for ever. "The end is where we start from..."

When Paul went back to Bramcote in September, I decided to join an evening class, rather than stay at home on my own. I didn't want anything too challenging, so 'creative writing', looked attractive. They were a really interesting group, terribly good at writing creatively, and they often read to the class the wonderful short stories, they had tossed off during the previous week. Our classroom was over a betting shop, which gave a faintly racy tinge to the meetings, and to my surprise they were very impressed by the fact that Giles and I had had textbooks actually 'published'. That was the key word, published.

I tried writing a short story, but I couldn't come up with anything that was even half as good as most of theirs. Then, watching children's telly one afternoon, I saw a Rupert Bear programme, with the narrative not in rhyme, It sounded so dull, after the bouncy style of the usual couplets and I assumed they had lost their script writer. I saw that a man named 'Trimble' had directed the film, so I wrote to him, in rhyme, hoping to catch his interest.

Dear Mr Trimble,

I declare, I'm worried about Rupert Bear.

He's been delighting girls and boys, with Annual's pleasures, comic's joys,

For years and years, and all this time, the narrative has been in rhyme,

And that was better, heaven knows, than current, rather stodgy, prose.

Perhaps there's been a problem, though, it seems a shame if this is so,

For someone, certainly, could write in verse, to put the matter right.

You see, that's what I'd like to do, if it would help the Bear and you,

So could I have a trial run, to prove to you that I'm the one?

Just let me have an outline plot, quite hard, to put me on the spot.

And I shall send right back to you, a sample of what I can do,

And hope to make the world aware, once more, of rhyming Rupert Bear.

So, Mr Trimble, hear my plea, and please do get in touch with me!

Jay Norris

I showed the 'letter' to the group and they loved it. I sent it to ITV, who had broadcast the Rupert Bear programme, asking for it to be forwarded to Mr Trimble. We were all very disappointed, when I didn't even get an acknowledgement!

I was dreading the first Christmas without Ernest, and suggested to Paul that we might go to Malta, which I had liked, when we called there, on one of the school cruises. He was not keen on the Mediterranean in December, but, going further afield, was a lot more expensive. Then Paul's undoubted luck and expertise, in the racing world, took over. He studied the form carefully and got up two big placepots, one at Newmarket, and the other at Redcar, and won over £1,500. Very generously, he offered to subsidise the holiday from his winnings, and take us both to certain sunshine in Sri Lanka and the Maldives.

If you have never ridden, in a bus, through the main streets of Colombo, you have been spared a very traumatic experience. Lots of cattle roaming aimlessly around, and everyone in a hurry and hooting their horns very loudly, does not make for a peaceful journey. Add to that, an apparent general suicidal urge to crash into another vehicle, and you can begin to know how we felt on the way to the Hotel Triton. It was a very good four star hotel, right on the shore and our room had a big balcony overlooking the sea. The straw beach umbrellas shaded very comfortable-looking sun beds, and we couldn't wait to start relaxing on them, with a good book and a cool drink.

After the inevitable buffet breakfast, we ventured out, good book in hand, to choose our spot for relaxation. There were very few people about, as it was quite early, but every sun-bed had a towel on it, suggesting that it had already been booked by someone else. It was disappointing, but we put our towels down on the sand, near one of the umbrellas, and enjoyed the lovely warm sun. I kept an eye on the beds, meaning to move onto one as soon as it was vacated, but no such luck. No one came to move the towels. I suggested to Paul that I should take two of the towels off, but he thought that might cause unpleasantness, when the owners returned.

By now, I had got interested in what was happening, and it was all too clear that, in order to have a sun-bed for an after lunch snooze, some people were bagging them early in the morning. I went to the reception desk and asked if the hotel management allowed this, and, of course, they didn't, so, together, we hatched a fiendish plan. Paul would give a pair of sandals to the beach attendants, who came on duty at six in the morning, and they would put them on the two chairs of our choice, very early, before the sun-bed baggers arrived. We would be playing the same selfish game but, at least, the beds would be used. Of course it worked well, and almost the best thing was the puzzled looks we got, when we were lying in the sun in comfort, from frustrated guests still holding their towels.

Sri Lanka was beautiful. Lush vegetation and lots of wild life. We hired a car, with driver, for a day, and he took us on a long, interesting tour. We saw the emerald mines and the baby turtle farm, and I was allowed to let one swim off, in the clear blue sea. We saw a bookies shop in a little village at the back of nowhere, and Paul went in to have a look inside. To his amazement, he found that they were betting on an English winter jump meeting. After a week at the Triton, we took a short flight to Male, in the Maldives, and began the second leg of our Christmas break. Because it is a chain of islands, every journey involves at least one crossing of the fairly rough sea. The little motor launch battled its way, for nearly an hour, to get us to our final destination, but it was worth it, when we saw our bungalow, right on the beach.

The package Paul had bought, included water sports, and he tried standing on a sail board, but it immediately sank, so we thought we'd better stick to snorkelling, eating the delicious food, all of which has to be brought in by sea, and drinking lots of alcohol, on our all-inclusive tariff. I have never drunk so many tots of Baileys Cream, in my life. The beaches were wonderful, with pale gold sand, and it was tempting to relax, and spend the time just sunbathing and having the odd swim in the clear blue, warm sea. We did a little voyage to another island, and it was an eye-opener, to see the native families, living in communities, with schools and markets, who supply the workers for the tourist trade. At the end of the week, we did the journey in reverse. First the motor launch to Male, then the flight to Colombo, and a transfer to the plane going to Manchester. The only hold-up was the awful 'jobsworth' behaviour of the airport security staff in Sri Lanka, Did they really think we were illegal immigrants?

Chapter 18

Back at 'Furlong House', I had one of my 'good ideas'. Such flashes of brilliance are not always appreciated by my immediate circle, and I remembered Ernest sighing and saying, "All right, what is it this time…?" I could buy a derelict cottage, have it renovated, and then use it as a third holiday let. We already had 'Furlong Cottage' and 'The Coach House Studio', but they were both attached to our home. This new part of the property folio, would be somewhere near the city centre, and would be for families. I casually mentioned the plan to Paul, and to my delight he was enthusiastic and positive. He would help with any mortgage arrangements, it would be a way of funding any future adventures, and let's start looking for somewhere straightaway. We scoured the local paper property section, but there was nothing suitable at a price we could afford.

Then, a local agent came up with a lovely little cottage, just a stone's throw from the city walls. In a quiet little mews, it backed on to an open space that had a children's playground, and would be perfect for tourist families. It was owned by a man who ran a pine furniture shop in York, but, interestingly, his mistress lived in it with their baby. She was a charming girl in her middle twenties, and I liked her immediately. She seemed perfectly content with her role in his life, and was clearly a loving mother to their new baby son. She showed me around, and it was just what we wanted. Better still, it needed very little renovation, and a cosmetic coat of paint would do the trick. We had easily found our new cottage. I started to look for the right furniture. It was like playing dolls' houses.

But, of course, it really was 'the best laid plans' scenario, all over again. Without warning, the vendor took the property off the market. The agent had no idea why, though he thought that there may have been a quarrel. I went to see the man at his shop, but he merely repeated his change of mind. I had to accept defeat. The only consolation was, as we found out later, that the open green space was taken over each evening by gangs of drinking teenagers, and the children's playground had to be closed, because it was so frequently vandalised.

I was driving near the new Tesco Superstore on the Tadcaster Road, when I spotted a little terraced house for sale. It was a mile or two out of town, but the recently opened 'Park & Ride', was close by. The road was reasonably busy, but there was a nice front garden, and a little shop, just two doors away. I went home, phoned the agent and arranged a viewing for that afternoon. I, immediately, thought it could be just right for us, as the price was only £45,000, but there was obviously a damp problem in several walls, and the bathroom was dire. There was a nice big sitting room, a back dining room, and a little, neglected kitchen. The bathroom was on the ground floor, and the two double bedrooms were up a steep flight of stairs. At the back of the house, a patio yard with a small shed had a back gate leading to a wonderfully secluded piece of countryside, around a large pond. Notices, from 'The Pond Committee', warned that fishing took place at one's own risk. Fishing? That sounded attractive, and the agent said that the pond was owned by the local council, and managed by volunteers. Even better, there was space behind the house for off road parking.

I called Paul, who came at once, and really liked the whole idea, so we made an offer, close to the asking price, and the house was ours. It seemed to take ages to put in a new damp course, replace the bathroom and the kitchen, install central heating, and get it decorated from top to bottom. We had the back patio attractively tiled, and I reorganised the front garden with some pretty flowering bushes. Replacement of the front windows with double glazing, the addition of blue wooden shutters and having the stucco façade painted white, finished the picture. True to form, we found a name, 'The Pond Cottage', and it was the first, of several similar acquisitions in our budding collection. We put it with our holiday agents, and it let extremely well.

Nothing daunted, when, the following year, two more of the terrace of four, came up for sale, we bought them, too, and, using Furlong House as security, there was no difficulty raising a lot of money. The other cottages got named, of course, 'Willow Cottage', for the house next door, and then Mike's suggestion, 'Mallard Cottage', for the last one. Holiday lets would have been too much hassle, so six month tenancies were perfect. Both were taken by attractive, single, young women, 'Willow' by a junior executive from M & S, and 'Mallard' by a student from Northern Ireland, who was studying at the York College of Law, and had a rich, estate agent father. Of course, the rents more than paid the mortgages.

Buying houses was such fun, and so profitable, that when we saw a former railway cottage, advertised for a bargain price, we just couldn't resist going to see it. It had a huge, overgrown garden, and was right by the actual main line, so that the trains shook the ground as they rushed by. Semi-detached, it was one of a pair, by a disused level crossing, and tucked down at the end of a quiet cul-de-sac. The company that owned it were rationalising their investments, and had set the price at a tempting £37,500, for a quick sale. We looked round it, called Steve, (our friend, the builder), who came at once, and thought it was a good buy, so there and then, we offered the asking price. The agent accepted on the spot, and so 'Trackside Cottage', as we named it, was ours. Interestingly, the downstairs bathroom, was, according to Steve, moving away from the rest of the building, and it actually had to be taken down and rebuilt. Serve it right!

I had ideas that we might be able to build a small detached cottage, on part of the garden, and we made a planning application. The plans, drawn up by Tony, the architect who had designed our coach house studio, looked exciting, and I had dreams that we might be on the way to making a small fortune. Alas, the application was turned down as the new building, they said, would be too near the railway line. We asked the agent about the cottage next to Trackside, and found that it was owned by the same company. It had a protected tenant, an old lady in her eighties, called Rose, whose husband had been a railwayman. We offered to buy it, with the tenant in situ, and they asked £30,000, rather more than we had hoped it would be, with a sitting tenant. However, they knew we wanted it, and refused to reduce the price, so I phoned Abbey National, and they agreed to take the total we owed them, up to a quarter of a million! Ernest must have been spinning around in his grave.

I called on Rose, and told her that we were her new landlords. She was relieved to hear that we were going to make several internal repairs that the big Newcastle owners had failed to do. We wanted her to be happy, and there were two other pieces of good news to cheer her up. Firstly, we were re-drawing the boundaries of the 'Trackside' garden, and her plot would be more than doubled in size, and, secondly, we were giving her house a name that we thought she would like. We wanted to keep the railway connection, and we were having a metal nameplate made at the railway workshop. The changes gave her a new lease of life, and she lived for several more years, enjoying the much bigger garden, which John, our gardener, made for her at 'Signalman's Cottage'. When 'Trackside' had been virtually rebuilt by Steve, it looked wonderful and we let it, unfurnished, for six months, but when those tenants moved to a house of their own, we sold it, at a small profit, and got ready for the next adventure. Buddy would have approved!

York was a great place to live, and by the time the grils were old enough, they sometimes came to stay at half term. From the time she was seven, Elizabeth often went on a three day course at the riding school, where children were given the experience of actually working in the stable. They forked out the old straw, (and everything it contained!), cleaned and polished the tack, fed and watered the ponies, and curry combed and brushed them till their coat shone. Then, as a reward, they went for a ride. It seemed a really good way to find out that, keeping a pony of your own, is very hard work.

Alex and Georgie, who weren't old enough for the riding school course, liked to go for the day to Merton, to the children's farm. We would take a picnic, and spend half the time defending our sandwiches against hungry ducks and goats, who seemed to think we had come especially to give them their lunch. We used to sing in the car, and their favourites were 'A keeper did a-hunting go' and 'Soldier, soldier, will you marry me?', which they rendered with great gusto. We really had fun, and sometimes we laughed so much that I had to park the car, till I stopped. I tried to behave like an affectionate grown-up, rather than a loving grandmother, as I wanted them to have fun, without any emotional hang-ups. Paul and I would often talk about friends we'd seen recently, and happened to mention Curly and his wife, Mary, who were coming to stay in the near future. Alex had been listening, and was clearly interested in this new name, so she asked, "Is Curlyanmary a boy or a girl?"

They always got a grade for how well they ate, a clean plate got A plus, and we took highly educational walks on the Knavesmire, identifying the different kinds of trees and flowers that we saw. Social training involved my friend, Lizzie, who lived a few houses away. She would have us to tea in her lovely home, and the Grils would behave beautifully. When we entertained, it was nearly always Father Hugh, from the church. We would bake fairy cakes for the occasion and they would put on white icing and a coloured inscription of 'I love FH', which always pleased him no end. We took them to mass one Christmas morning and Father Hugh got rather carried away with his Christmas message. It did seem to be longer than usual, and little Georgina's voice rang out quite clearly, "How many more hours is it?"

Of course, unwittingly they did and said things that were very endearing. We went to the crematorium garden one year, on June 1st, Ernest's anniversary, to lay some flowers beside the little golf hole in which his ashes had been buried. I could not help crying quietly when I thought of him, and it made the Grils very sad. They started to speak about how much they had loved him, even though I was fairly sure that the person they went on to describe, certainly wasn't Ernest. As their imaginations ran riot, involving someone who had told them stories as they sat on his knee, who had played with them, and had given them hugs, the inventions got so unlike the real Ernest, that they made me laugh, and we got back to 'Furlong House' with our cheerfulness restored.

They shared one of our guest rooms, which had bunk beds that always got smothered with dollies and teddies at bedtime. Elizabeth, as the oldest, had the top bunk to herself, and the other two were end to end at the bottom. I would read them a story, tuck them in, kiss them all, turn out the light and go downstairs. They were as good as gold, and quickly went to sleep, waking early the next day, ready for action. I really enjoyed having them, and missed little voices saying, “What oo doing, Day?”, when I had taken them back to London.

The Bramcote Centenary in 1993, brought the next interesting project for Paul. Many of the parents had racing connections and it was decided to lease a racehorse, name it ‘Bramcote Centenary’, and run it at northern flat meetings. The name would be printed in the racing runners and riders section of every newspaper which would be good sales promotion for the school, and it would be an extra bonus, if it won a race. More importantly, everyone would have a great deal of fun. Racing colours were selected, the red and white hoops of the school’s rugby shirts, and an attractive little two year old filly, was chosen and was trained at a yard near Malton. Sadly, she went lame on the gallops, so a second filly, named ‘Bramcote Century’, took her place. Her first run was to be at Thirsk, a lovely open course, near the centre of this attractive little market town, and the school would sponsor a race. Paul suggested that we might also have a race and call it ‘The Ernest Norris Memorial Handicap’, and we could share the refreshment marquee with Bramcote. Racing is, very much, a social event, and I thought that Ernest would have loved the idea. Several of the parents had met ‘Paul’s dad’, so the whole thing worked out well. So well, in fact, that we repeated the experiment the following year.

I really preferred the country racecourse, just outside Beverley, a lovely old town with a beautiful Minster, so when it looked as though Ernest’s race would become an annual event, I asked Paul if we could transfer our sponsorship there. The Chairman of the Course, Charlie M, was also a Bramcote parent, an absolutely charming man, with a very attractive wife, named Ros. He invited us to share the ‘Chairman’s Box’ with him, and our friends could enjoy a champagne lunch. There was a balcony overlooking the winning post and the view of the races was superb. We were all given badges to take us into the Members’ Enclosure, and placards were put outside the racecourse entrance, welcoming “The Family and Friends of the late Ernest Norris”. We felt we had made sure that he would not be forgotten by the rest of world.

Before the race, there was the sponsor's 'Best turned-out' award, and it was judged as the runners walked around the paddock. Having absolutely no idea what we were looking for, we needed the advice of guests like Nicky and Ali, who knew all about horses, before we could pick the winner of the cash prize. James got to present the envelope to the winning stable lad, or lass, and he was always glad when it was a pretty girl, who could be given a congratulatory kiss. We chose the guests very carefully.

Every year we invited family, James and Karen, and Giles, plus close friends like Jan and Mike with Charlie, and, of course Nigel and Nicky. They all travelled from London to York, and it was great to see them, so that gave an extra fillip to the occasion. Then there would be several friends, like Father Hugh, who were important in our lives at that particular moment, so the guest list differed each year. The Chairman's guests were also lunching with us, so we met some very interesting people, loosely connected to racing. It was a very enjoyable social occasion, and as our race was run at the June meeting, we nearly always had good weather.

The race itself often seemed an anti-climax. Each year, Paul presented a bronze statuette of a horse and jockey to the winning owner, suitably engraved, so the name 'Ernest Norris', must appear in the trophy cabinets of owners all over the world. The winning jockey was given a bottle of champagne, and one year it went to Willie Carson, who had already had four winners that afternoon. Apparently, he was so tired by the time he won our race, that he nearly didn't make it to the winners' enclosure to collect his prize.

We all betted modestly on the afternoon's races, and the one really big win went to Jan, who chose number 5 in every race. Expecting a small return from the Tote when her horse won, she found the clerk worried by mistakenly having given Jan a £5 ticket, when she had only paid for a £2 bet. Would Jan mind paying the other £3 to put the books straight, before she received her winnings? Being Jan, she immediately agreed to help by paying the balance, and she was amazed when she won over £300 on the new bet. We were all delighted! Sometimes, in the middle of all the fun, I would feel so sad that Ernest wasn't there to enjoy his very own race. He would have loved it.

Chapter 19

We all thought that Tala Mai, Cliff's villa in Portugal, was perfect, but, for him it had one big disadvantage. It was right beside a little winding path, that ran down to the sea, and so someone in the pool, or playing tennis, or just sunbathing, could be clearly seen over the low wall by the path. No one bothered to try to get a good look of any of us, but for Cliff himself it was different. Once the fans knew where the loved one could be seen in flesh and blood, they came to look, and his privacy was invaded, so he tried to find something more secluded. He heard of a farmhouse for sale, with a pool, a tennis court, and several acres of land, so he went to see it, and after a little negotiation on the price, bought it. Quite a lot of work would have to be done to renovate the main house and the caretaker's bungalow, which had both been rather neglected, but it ticked all the boxes of Cliff's needs, and proved to be a wonderful buy.

We were staying at 'Tala Mai', in 1992, when Cliff's purchase of the Quinta do Moinho, as it was called, went through, so we drove over to see it. There were huge wrought iron gates with a drive leading up to the house, but we managed to get the caretaker to let us in, to see around the garden. An old man and his wife were shaking the fruit from the olive trees, on to sacking that had been laid on the ground. It was like a scene from a film about peasant life in rural Portugal in the olden days. We wandered around the grounds, noting that the swimming pool tiles were covered in bright green algae, but that there were orange, lemon and fig trees, and huge pink and purple bougainvillea vines climbed everywhere. We fell in love with The Quinta, at first sight. Of course, we realised that it would probably not be ready for Booker Prize unofficial committee meetings, for the following year, so we decided to rent something in the south of France, to fill the gap. Paul saw an advertisement in The Times, about a villa in Biot, in Provence, which sounded a perfect stopgap, so we booked it, though it was not the millionaire's paradise in Portugal, that we were used to!

Biot is in the Alpes Maritimes, about five miles from the Mediterranean, and was once the home of Fernand Leger, whose designs and pottery were world famous. There is a museum, displaying his work, with some spectacular sculptures in the garden. The villa was very comfortable, with a big open fire, that was a definite necessity on chilly November evenings, and we stoked it so enthusiastically, that we set fire to the wooden beam that ran across the chimney breast. The swimming pool had a brick wall down one side, but the water was so cold that only Richard went in more than once. There was a main sitting area, with a little room leading off it, that Jan called 'Badger's Den', which was a wonderfully quiet place to catch up on our studies of the short-listed books. We went to visit Cannes, Monte Carlo and Antibes, as well as charming little hill villages, tucked away, well off the tourist trail. The things I remember best are, that we all thoroughly enjoyed Provence, that one supermarket, near Antibes, was so big that the assistants rode around on roller skates, and that 'Paddy Clark Ha Ha Ha', won the Booker Prize.

The main disadvantage that came from living in the north of England, was that my most of my friends lived in the south, and though they made valiant efforts to keep in touch, it was a long journey if they came on a visit. I had gone to watch a rehearsal for one of Cliff's concerts when I was in London, and he and Bill took me, for lunch, to a barge moored near Canary Wharf. The food was delicious, the location quite exciting, and it was a private restaurant. It was so good, in fact, that when I got back to York, I rang them to see what it would cost to hire it for an evening dinner party, and when I realised it was within my price range, I made plans to book it. There was just one oblong table, with only twenty-two chairs, so I had to work out who, in my 'Wall of Friendship', I could invite, make a table seating plan, and send out the invitations. I checked with Cliff, when he would be free, and we fixed a date.

The first dinner on 'The Barge', proved one thing beyond doubt: as an idea, it was a corker. We started with a champagne reception, ate a delicious four course meal, with wine, and then, as the liqueurs were being sipped, I made a little speech, welcoming the guests. We all talked our heads off, and not only did I get to see my friends, but they got to see each other. It was a recipe for success, and the format has remained pretty much the same, from then on. The first barge closed in 1995, but the one moored next to it, took over, and we have been having dinner parties there ever since. Linda, the delightful Scottish owner, enters into the spirit of the whole thing, and she always produces a menu, emblazoned with the Wall of Friendship logo, to mark the occasion.

One main change, however, has been the dress code. Originally, it was, to borrow a phrase from Cunard, ' smart-casual', which created insecurities in the what-to-wear stakes, but a switch to 'black tie', solved the problem permanently. I think that men look wonderfully attractive in DJ's, and women very sexy in evening outfits, and formal dress certainly helped to make The Barge seem a very special occasion.

In 2008, to celebrate Cliff's 50th Year in showbiz, we all sported a touch of gold. Paul bought me a very sparkly gold jacket from Ebay, and I would not have looked out of place, hanging on a Christmas tree. There were several 'new' faces, as John and Mary travelled all the way from Ireland, the Boyz, our friends from France came hurrying through the tunnel, and Derek brought Mu with him, from North Wales.

Cliff's book, "My Life, My Way", had just appeared, and, very generously, the publisher had sent a copy for everyone at the dinner, so we started the evening with a signing session. Jan and Mike organised the distribution of the books, Cliff signed them and Paul took a picture to mark each event. It was a real production line, that worked well, without exhausting the author, and, at the champagne reception, it was lovely to welcome Penny Junor, who had ghosted this fascinating book. Paul played a ukelele, bought specially for the occasion, and we sang a revised version of 'Congratulations' to Cliff, for we certainly wanted 'the world to know, we're happy as can be!" The Wall of Friendship dinners are, indeed, my attempt to say thank you, to the most wonderful group of friends anyone could wish for.

Spending an evening with Cliff, it is always difficult for me to remember that he is no longer a boy. I can never quite take in the metamorphosis of 'Harry', from Room 9, into Sir Cliff Richard, the most successful British pop star ever. It is only when I compare the photos of then and now, that I even realise that he looks a little older. He has managed to be unspoilt by fame, and is a wonderful example of how to stay genuinely likeable. I was absolutely delighted when he was knighted for his services to charity, as I knew that he was very generous in his support of 'Tear Fund', which did wonderful work in deprived areas of the third world. He took long and exhausting journeys to see the workers on the ground, and it made a huge difference to them to have his reassuring and cheerful presence.

The passing of the years is not always so kind. Paul and I went on a holiday in California, and by the pool, was an old lady, sitting in the shade. The air was quite chilly and I thought she might be feeling cold, so I offered to move her chair into the sun. "Why no, dear," she said, in a wonderful southern accent, "I never sit in the sun, because it ruins your skin", she gave me a long look, and added, "but then you know that already." I think my reaction would be best described as, 'collapse of stout party!'

The struggle against wrinkles and sags, seems to be a losing battle, and the creams that suggest they can restore the look of youth, should be prosecuted under the 'Trade's Description Act'.

THE ANTI-AGEING CREAM LAMENT

One tenet of my life now seems
To trust in anti-ageing creams,
Yet such naivety defies
The evidence before my eyes.

Instruction leaflets make it clear
That lines will shortly disappear,
But, sadly, I report to you,
This information isn't true

Now someone's told me it's the rage
To blame the sun, and not your age.
While gravity can cause that frown
By years and years of dragging down.

So, maybe, now it's all too late,
I must, for once, accept my fate,
For even Botox, though sublime,
Can't hide the ravages of time.

But I feel young inside, and so
I'm letting every mirror go,
And I'll make sure there's not a doubt,
I'll see myself as inside out!

In 1994, we had the excitement of an autumn break in a wonderful new setting, for Cliff told me that the renovation of 'The Quinta' had been completed, and he would be happy to let us use it at half term. We were thrilled to bits, and I asked my friends, Lizzie and John, who lived on Mount Vale, to come with us. She had been a real help when I was struggling to get over the loss of Ernest, and had just taken some qualification to become a marriage guidance counsellor. When I heard the long, tedious and time-consuming route to reconciliation, I was frankly amazed, "Why not just tell them what's wrong, and how to put it right?" Lizzie laughed, and told me it didn't work like that, so we agreed that I should cross 'marriage-guidance' off my list of prospective future careers. John was a judge, and, once he was sure that accepting the invitation wouldn't prejudice any future court proceedings, they were happy to join the party.

This time it truly was a millionaire's paradise. Everything in the house was wonderful, and even the caretaker now had his own pool. The main pool was magnificent, the edges enlivened by statues representing the four seasons, fountains sparkled in the sun, the garden beds were full of exotic plants, and hand- painted tiles, that high spot of Portuguese art, decorated every wall and table top. Breakfast on the immense patio, the wrought iron chairs silhouetted against the dazzlingly white walls of the house, was so picturesque that cameras were always at the ready, and "Say cheese!" became the order of the day.

There was a magnificent kitchen, with a huge stove and hotplate, a microwave, a dishwasher and spacious fridges. Very comfortable dining chairs were set around the big table that became the social centre of the house for us. It was there that we ate dinner, played 'O Hell', and gossiped, once it began to get dark. French doors led out on to a balcony that overlooked the orange grove and gave a distant view of the sea. There was even a formal dining room, but we only used it for the final meeting of the unofficial Booker committee, when we voted on which book should win, if only the official committee had some sense. The four double bedrooms, each had a spacious adjoining bathroom, and everywhere was sparklingly clean and bright. Cliff had his own suite of rooms, overlooking the pool, so we did not feel we were intruding into his private space, which was reassuring.

The weather was fine and warm, and we read our books, sitting on the comfortable sun loungers by the pool, and some of the men played the occasional game of tennis, on the spanking new court. We did innumerable wine-tastings under the shade of the bougainvillea vines, and had a competition to see who could spot the most expensive vintage. John did very well, and also turned out to be a good card player, when we taught him 'O, Hell'. His book was 'How Late It Was How Late', a novel set in Glasgow, which had gained a doubtful notoriety, by using the 'f-word' a record number of times. Lizzie had the beautifully written, 'Knowledge of Angels', which I thought should win, but, true to form, the official Booker Committee gave the prize to the f-book!

Altogether, it was a really enjoyable week. John and Lizzie fitted in extremely well, and Jan and I talked our heads off, as usual, frequently getting the giggles. Paul cooked wonderful food, and Richard, Giles and Mike shamed the rest of us by bravely swimming in the lovely, but slightly chilly, pool. A garden path led down to a large field, where grape vines had been planted, and it was clear that Cliff was getting really interested in the possibilities of making his own wine. In fact, the first appearance of 'Vida Nova' was only a few years away, by which time he had bought more land, and was running a successful commercial venture.

The new caretaker, Carlos, had an English wife, he had met in Newcastle, where he had worked as a barman. They had a dear little girl, who toddled everywhere, so their swimming pool had to be enclosed, to stop her falling in. Sadly, we heard later, that life in Portugal had proved difficult: Carlos's wife got homesick, so she took their little daughter back to England, and the marriage ended.

I picked up my busy life in York, and there were so many things to do, that I found it hard to avoid defeat in the allotment battle against a weed called 'mare's tail'. My efforts to grow my own asparagus had failed, and it would have been much easier, and a lot cheaper, to have had it delivered daily from Fortnum & Mason's. We had found good friends in Rodger and Ruth, whose talented sons had been at Bramcote, and who lived in a beautiful old farmhouse near Beverley. Every few weeks, Rodger and his mother, Joan, would make up a bridge four with us. We would have the most delicious supper at their great big farmhouse table, as Ruth was a cordon bleu cook. Then we would sit and play some very competitive rubber bridge. I really liked Joan, who was very warm and charming, played a very good game of cards, and was great fun to talk to.

I had taken Rosie, our collie-cross, to dog training, but she still ran off, unpredictably, and would not come back when she was called. I had found a new dog-loving friend in Ali, one of the Bramcote parents, who lived, with her three children, quite near, in a fashionable square. She had a Jack Russell, appropriately called 'Jack', and she suffered the same dog disobedience as I did, but she was much nicer about it. I could, quite cheerfully, have killed Rosie, when, in cold, wet weather, I called in vain for her to come back. Ali and I went for long walks on the Knavesmire, and I told her about some of my friends, especially Giles, and hoped that one day I could introduce them to each other. They really had so much in common that I was certain they would get on very well.

It happened that Paul decided to have a dinner party for his birthday in 1995, and we invited Mike and Jan, and also Giles, to come and stay. It was just the opportunity I had been waiting for and I asked Ali to join us. I hoped for fireworks, 'light the blue touch paper and retire', and I wasn't disappointed. The meal was delicious, the wine brought a feel good factor, and all through dinner we could sense that there was a mutual attraction. When the end of the evening came, at about midnight, Giles offered to walk Ali home. Paul said he would stay up to let him in, and advised him to take Rosie, as she would show him the way home. Paul went to bed at two, but got up at three, when Giles rang the bell to be let in. There was a weak story about Rosie leading him astray, but we brushed that aside, and, some time later, Ali moved to London. I had lost my 'walkies' companion, but I was really happy for my two dear friends, and over the moon, when, five years later, they married.

A year later, Cliff got his 'Midsummer Night's Dream' wish. He played Heathcliff, in a musical adaptation of 'Wuthering Heights'. He asked me if I would like to bring some friends, and we could all go out to dinner, after the show. I invited Nigel and Nicky, Charlie M and Ros, from Beverley and Father Hugh. Charlie M drove us up to Nigel's beautiful house in Essex, where we were to spend the night, and then we went, in convoy, to the Apollo Victoria theatre in London. I was slightly nervous about seeing the show. I wondered how Emily Bronte might have felt, to see the agony of the Cathy/Heathcliff love affair, set to pop music.

There was a single set, made up of several levels, artistically disguised as grassy hillocks. The huge theatre was packed, and there was an audible gasp, when a bearded Cliff appeared. Cathy was a pretty woman, with a nice voice, but I thought that it was when Heathcliff came on stage, that the real drama started to happen. It was not an easy role to take on, and Cliff was playing well out of his comfort zone, but he managed to be the rough, demanding lover that the story demanded. I breathed a sigh of relief, as I had been afraid that I might not like it. The conversation at dinner would not have to be guarded comments, on an 'interesting' performance.

The final curtain brought tumultuous applause and Cliff stepped forward, raising a hand to get silence. He said, "This has been a very special evening." It crossed my mind that we had been really lucky to be there at such a time, then he continued, "Jay Norris is here", and went on to tell the audience how, at school, I had introduced him to the book. In the applause that followed, everyone looked around for this special person, so I looked around too, but I couldn't spot her anywhere. When we met later in the restaurant, Cliff said he hoped I hadn't minded his announcement, as he had worried whether I would like the show. I gave him a big hug, and told him about my doubts, which had, happily, proved to be totally unfounded. I thought 'Heathcliff' had made a really entertaining and successful evening. His 'dream' had, finally, come true.

We spent the night at 'Little Laver Hall', Nigel's impressive home, and I was pleased to hear that Charlie M and Ros had enjoyed meeting Cliff, and had liked the show. Father Hugh thought that the music had been quite difficult to put over, but that my friend, Cliff, had done very well. The next morning at breakfast, the air was filled with the wonderful smell of homemade bread, from Nicky's new breadmaking machine, and we made the journey back to York on Cloud 9. It had, definitely, been an enjoyable visit to the south.

Chapter 20

Every time we went on holiday in France, I was all too aware that my French was definitely not fluent. I watched with envy as Mike, who had lived for a time in Paris, chatted easily to everyone he met. Paul spoke excellent French, and had absolutely no problems in relating to all and sundry. Despite being educated at a convent school, where almost all the nuns were French, I was pathetic. It really annoyed me, and I kept meaning to do something about it. The opportunity arose when I saw an advertisement in the York local paper for classes in French, run by Alliance Français, covering beginner, intermediate and advanced students. I reckoned they ought to be able to fit me in, somewhere in that range. I went to the official enrolment and, to my relief, I was rated 'intermediate', and joined the group, led by a lively, young French teacher, named Catherine.

There were nine of us, and we met in a classroom at a local school, on Wednesday afternoons, and, very quickly, we bonded into a viable unit. I particularly liked Ursula, who lived in a house next to the Ouse, and so got flooded out every year, and Pam, who was a talented artist and had shows of her work in places like Edinburgh. Catherine was always encouraging, but tried to stop us chatting merrily away in English , with little cries of "En français!", and I soon learnt that the French for 'to gossip', was 'bavarder!'

Each week we were asked to report on what we had done since we last met, in connected, grammatical sentences. Not as easy as it sounds. We then looked at the new words the reader had used, and added them to our vocabulary lists. One week, Clare spoke of the squirrel, l'écureil, she had seen in the park, and Sal, who had been to Monet's garden, enthused about les nénuphars, the water lilies. I dutifully jotted them down in my notebook, and thought what fun it would be to make a rhyme, as a way of remembering some of the more awkward words. I offered the idea to the class, with the two new words as a starter.

"Voila, l'écureuil est là, et il regarde les nénuphars!"

To my slight surprise, they loved it, and so every week, from then on, I was expected to produce a little verse, to include the previous week's more interesting vocabulary. The good thing, from my point of view, was that the 'poem', as they called it, took the place of the report, I would otherwise, have had to write, and it was a lot more fun to do. I bought a little book of French light verse, and because the word endings tend to be repeated, it was certainly not too difficult to find a rhyming sequence. Catherine got quite interested in an idea that I had for a text book, that would use simple verses to teach idiomatic French phrases to children, and we met a couple of times to discuss whether or not it would work. However, she was busy, looking after her new baby, and I was already on to the next project, so nothing came of it. Rather a pity, as it would have been very interesting to do.

We ended our first term with a Christmas lunch at a restaurant in York, which was very jolly and it was a relief to talk to each other in English. I had written a little poem, as a sort of 'franglais' Christmas card, and gave a copy to each of them at the end of the meal. The words in French, were the ones that had cropped up in reports during the term, and it had been done on Paul's computer, so it was set out nicely, with a funny little snowman, decorating the title.

GETTING INTO FRENCH

Just once a week, *le mercredi, le groupe* A.F. in York,
Has met *apprendre le français. Ecoute! Ecrire! Et* talk!

There's Ursula, *et* Pat, *et* Sue, *et* Joyce, *et* Sal, *et* Jay;
And Clare, and Pam, and Susan, too; a chance *de bavarder.*

De temps en temps we've noted down *l'histoire de chaque ménage,*
From *vide pomme* to *pneu dégonflé*, and search for *coquillage.*

Sous les étoiles; feu d'artifice; les chiens we love so dear;
Le clochard et la dépanneuse, they go *de mal en pire.*

Et Catherine, *notre professeur*, fulfils our every want,
She's *authentique*, and *à la mode*, so truly *épatante.*

Her guidance through *'Grammaire Eclat'* would win the Booker Prize,
Et elle se met en quatre. (Note the effort that implies!)

But term must end and *"Au revoir!"* will be the final cry,
Nous allons glacer nos gâteaux, but still it's not goodbye,

En janvier, we start again to work with *Alliance*,
And we'll be there, once more to say, *"Bonjour!"*
et VIVE LA FRANCE!

JOYEUX NOEL et BONNE ANNEE !!

We finished the year together, and I certainly felt my vocabulary had greatly improved by the end, but Catherine went back to teaching full time, and the group broke up. Well, c'est la vie!

It was about this time that we seriously thought of buying a little holiday cottage in Normandy. On holiday with Jan and Mike in Villers-sur-mer, a seaside town about five miles from Deauville, we thought that we might be able to afford to buy a cottage, that we could stay in, or let, for the races. We could sell one of our York properties, and have a second home in France. It was a very attractive thought, as prices were lower in Villers than they were in York, and the town had all the things we would want. There was a daily market for foodstuffs, and a weekly big event, when stalls filled the church square, selling clothes and everything else under the sun. It was, essentially, a French resort, that did not seem to attract British tourists, and we checked the car licence plates to make sure. There were plenty of little inexpensive cafes, a casino with a bridge club, and a lovely sandy beach. What more could we want?

We went to all the local estate agents and explained what we were looking for. They seemed moderately interested, and promised to let us know, if anything suitable turned up. Then, the holiday over, we drove to Ouistreham for the Portsmouth ferry, and the long trek back to York. We waited, impatiently, for news from the immobiliers in Villers, but nothing came. Paul telephoned, but with no result. We got absolutely nowhere, and our opinion of the French estate agencies hit rock bottom.

It was in May, that the Yorkshire Show Ground, just outside Harrogate, hosted 'The French Property Show', a gathering of British-based agents, intent on selling houses in France, to, in this instance, the people of North Yorkshire. We went on a whim, not expecting any result after Villers, but interested in seeing where else might be worth investigating. We found the show ground without any problem, and there were quite a few exhibitors offering properties in the Cote d'Azur or the Dordogne, favourite watering holes for many ex-pats. We were interested in properties on the Normandy coast, and those that were not too far from Calais, like Le Touquet.

There seemed to be some pleasant, inexpensive houses available in Picardy, so we took lots of details, with photos, though, when we showed them to friends, everyone picked the same house as their favourite. It was in a village near Abbeville, detached, with four bedrooms, and a large garden with 'outbuildings'.

Our visit to 'Goléo', the local agency, was an echo of the Villers experience. When we got to Abbeville, they were sorry but the owners of the house we were interested in were away, but they had other properties we could see. We asked for the address, but in line with the policy of not telling anyone anything that is the mantra of French agents, they would not reveal the location. We said we would like to look at it from the outside, so they agreed to show us that, en route to seeing other properties nearby.

When we, finally, got to the house, lo and behold, there were two people standing in the large front garden, and the agent recognised them as the English owners. They had not been away, but were out to lunch when the agent called, and they would be happy to show us round. To cut a long story short, we loved it on sight, and to everyone's amazement, offered to buy it. We found out, later, that the house had been on the market for four years and they had almost despaired of finding a buyer. We signed the 'compromis de vente' the next day, and went back to York, bubbling with excitement.

Everyone wanted to know all about our new venture, so we had to give it a name. A line of little rose trees ran by either side of the front path, and Paul suggested, 'Les Rosiers', the rose bushes, so that was settled. We had already booked a cottage in Courcelles, in Normandy, for our August holiday, and had asked Mike and Jan to join us. We were able to tell them that the final signing for 'Les Rosiers', would be just as we would be leaving France, so on our way home, we could all go together to Goléo's, for the official completion of the sale. We had cash, and the huge investigation that precedes every sale in France, went through without a hitch.

In 'French Property News', required reading for British owners, I had seen an advertisement for a firm of architects, offering advice on the renovation of older properties in Northern France. Definitely, we were going to have to do some work on the main building, and on the dilapidated maison d'amis. There was also a ruined barn in the grounds, needing to be totally rebuilt, if it was to be of any use, whatsoever. I spoke to Philip, who had a calm, reassuring voice, and arranged for us to meet him at 'Les Rosiers', after the final signing in August.

We had a great holiday in Courcelles, enlivened by a health scare, when Mike paid the price of bravely trying some brawn, at a slightly tacky restaurant, and we travelled to Abbeville for the 'Acte de vente', that would make 'Les Rosiers' legally ours. Monsieur Goléo, the owner of the agency, was there in person, and both Jan and I thought that he was a very strange fellow, bright eyed and bushy tailed, but...? We couldn't quite decide what. Once the long, tedious procedure, in which every page of the document had to be signed separately, was over, we whizzed off to Allery, our village, to show 'Les Rosiers' to Jan and Mike, and to meet Philip.

The previous owners were there to hand over the keys, and had already moved out their furniture, except for the one or two things we were buying from them, like beds and the kitchen table. We did a quick tour with Mike and Jan, and we were all amazed at how big the house felt, now it was empty. The garden looked fine, but Paul was already thinking that we would have to buy a sit-on mower, for the front and back lawns. I couldn't quite believe that we actually owned this huge property, but plans to make it even bigger, were already forming in my mind. It needed a conservatory, to lead out of the kitchen, and join the glass veranda that went right across the back of the house. That should, definitely, be our first construction priority.

We were exploring the garden, when Philip arrived, and he proved to be as calm and unhurried, as he had sounded on the telephone. Slowly rolling his own cigarettes, he gave his initial reaction to the state of the building. The roof, it appeared, was 'weary', though he liked the house's mid-Victorian style and thought we had made a reasonably good investment. He went round the maison d'amis, in which the previous owners had stored their garden tools, and said that he could give us practical advice on its complete restoration. He took a great shine to Mike, and we all liked him, so he became 'our architect'. Our new role, as property owners in France, had well and truly begun.

The actual renovation of the house took quite a long time, and quite a lot of money. Every one helped us. Derek and I were taken over, one weekend, by John the gardener in his van. We took some more furniture, as well as the china and the linen and the kitchen equipment that was needed to set up home. We cleaned out cupboards, and hoovered and swept and dusted, till the place was liveable-in. Then Paul joined us and we started all over again. Exhausted at the end, we drank some very good wine and slept soundly.

In school holidays, the exploration of the area became an enjoyable extra-curricular activity. Paul thought that the countryside around the Somme valley was very like the dales in the north of England, with lakes and gently rolling hills, and the sea only thirty miles away, at ports like Mers-les Bains and Le Tréport. William the Conqueror had set sail from Saint Valéry-sur-Somme, in 1066, and Le Touquet was not too far away for an evening's gambling at the Casino. It was even easy to do a tour of the Somme battlefields to the south.

The actual village of Allery, was well spread-out, along the back road to the little town of Airaines, and was, basically, agricultural. The road was labelled 'Route du Lait', and, sure enough, there were cows grazing peacefully behind the farm buildings. The one and only shop was almost opposite our house, and sold almost everything from butter and plants, to children's clothes. It had a lot of shelves but not a lot of stock, so each piece of merchandise was displayed with space all round it, as though quarantined because of some mysterious infection.

Properties in Allery, ranged from a stately maison de maître, with huge iron gates, used by the German Commandant during the Occupation, to shacks that looked totally unsuitable for human habitation. There was a spacious 'mairie' for the mayor, with an impressive war memorial for a service each November 11th, when the names on the side would be read out as "Mort pour la France", after which, the village band had played a rather shaky tune, just recognisable as the Marseillaise. As Paul's Australian client, Bruce, would have said, "It all looks so French!"

We spent our first Christmas holidays there in 2000, and went to look for a glass company, to add a conservatory to the back of the house. It was Boxing Day, but we found a firm, on the industrial outskirts of Abbeville, who promised to send someone to give us an estimate. They asked if we knew the English builders who lived in the district, and when we said we didn't, they gave us a number to phone. And that is how we got to know The Boyz. We invited them to come and see us, and when we met them we were sure that we had found the two people who would, when we were back in York, be able to carry out the various alterations we had in mind. They had a good look round the house, inspected the maison d'amis, and photographed the ruined barn. There was going to be a lot to do, and we asked them to plan for a busy year ahead. I was very relieved that they were English, so I wouldn't have to learn the French words for conditions like, rising damp and blocked drains, that might crop up in the future.

Paul had been very upset by the death of John G, the Bramcote deputy head, in the previous summer holidays, and he began to feel that, perhaps, the time had come to leave teaching, and try something else. He spoke fluent French, he was interested in property, and had, what are often called, good people skills. We knew, from bitter experience, that agents in France, were not really interested in searching out houses for foreign clients, which was really surprising, as they stood to gain fees of up to seven or eight percent, if they made a sale. Paul could fill the gap, as a consultant, finding properties for individual English-speaking buyers, and guarding their interests, against any French intransigency. He had to find a name for the new company, and after several tries, settled on 'Right In France', which he hoped people wouldn't misconstrue, as support for Jean-Marie Le Penn, the Nationalist leader. So, after one particularly cold and rainy lesson on the games field in Scarborough, Paul decided the time had come to try life in France, and handed in his resignation.

We immediately put 'Furlong House' up for sale, and started to plan for the future. I was determined to keep a base in England, so the immediate question was, where should that base be? We needed easy access to the Channel ports and to Eurotunnel, so our house-hunting would be in south Kent, and I watched the property advertisements in the Sunday papers, with great interest. The good news was that prices in our chosen area seemed reasonable, and I knew Folkestone and Dover, from our visits to Pam and Den, when they lived in Saltwood. I had liked the rolling hills of the Kentish Weald, and the elegant outline of the occasional oast house, in the many pretty villages. Hythe, where the Norman parish church had a spectacular collection of human bones, was the home of my friend, Toffee: who was so-called because her surname was 'Sharp', and the old advertising slogan had insisted that, "Sharp's the word for Toffee". Her real name was 'Marjorie', but she hated it so much, that even her family called her 'Peggy'. I hoped that, if we came to live near Hythe, I would often see her.

Finally, one Sunday, there was just the kind of house we were looking for, advertised for sale. A grade 2 listed cottage, in a village near Ashford, at a price we could afford. It sounded perfect, so I rang the number, hoping to have a chat with the owner. It turned out to be the number of an estate agent, which was useful, as I wanted to know a lot more about property in that part of Kent. I spoke to Val, who answered all my questions with great patience, and by the time the conversation was over, I had arranged to come down from York, and spend a day, seeing several houses, including the cottage. We met at her office, and she had made several appointments to view houses, in both morning and afternoon. I couldn't help thinking how very much better English estate agents are, than their French counterparts. She was confident that I would find exactly what I was looking for, in the wide selection she was offering, and she was, as ever, right!

The grade 2 cottage had low ceilings, very charming but unsuitable for six foot five Paul, and a smart, renovated barn had lovely high ceilings, but was in the middle of nowhere. We hadn't considered a new build, but Val recommended the work of a firm called 'Rogate', who specialised in well-designed properties, in excellent locations. They had just finished a new development in Hythe, and everything was already sold. Val suggested that we should go and look at it, as she was sure I would be impressed by the very high quality of the fixtures and fittings. The location certainly was perfect, right next to Waitrose, Paul's favourite supermarket, and all the houses were attached, but different in shape and size, to give the appearance of a medieval village. What a pity that they were all sold.

The largest property was on the corner of the development, looking out over the sweeping lawns that bordered the Military Canal, and it had a name, 'Wellington House'. Val told me it had been the first to be sold, off-plan, but workmen were just adding the finishing touches, so we could have a look round. Rogate employed Sue, a very personable sales hostess, and we had an enjoyable tour of the house with her, noting, of course, the high quality of everything.

The sitting room was on the first floor, and the big bay window gave a superb view of the parish church up on the hill. There were two double bedrooms on the second floor, one with an ensuite shower room, and the kitchen-dining room, on the ground floor, was next to a useful little study. What a pity it was already sold as it would have suited us beautifully. So far, we had been, without question, very lucky in the houses we have owned, 'Wits End', 'Little Gidding' and 'Furlong House,' all just happened to come on the market, at the exactly the right moment for us. In fact, our guardian angel was on the ball yet again, as the off-plan buyer for 'Wellington House' reneged on the deal, so, gratefully, we immediately bought it.

Chapter 21

After the usual hiccups, that, by now, we almost expected, Furlong House had been bought by some people I really liked. This is always a bonus when you are selling a house in which you have been very happy, and I had handed over the keys, knowing that they would love living there. The move to Hythe was simple, as we were buying modern furniture for the new house, so we took very little with us.

Rosie, our dog, had died of old age, and Jacques, the pedigree-cross collie puppy, we had bought to keep her company, was wonderfully obedient and well-behaved. We would miss the Knavesmire for walks, but it would be replaced by the equally green, green, grass of The Grove. A lovely surprise awaited us in Hythe, because Giles and Ali turned up in the afternoon, with a bottle of champagne, to wish us good luck in 'Wellington House'. Now we had two places to live, one in England and one in France, so my itching feet had been well and truly scratched!

Hythe proved to be a very good choice, for a pied-a-terre. It had every shop we needed in the narrow, old High Street, and I found a wonderful hairdresser, called Angela, who did everything possible to keep me looking reasonably with it! The sea was a mere five minute stroll away, across the Military Canal, which got quite crowded in the summer. There were little rowing boats full of excited families, and patient fishermen sitting for hours on end, on the steep banks, with their rods dipping into the water, but their keep-nets, apparently, empty. The canal dated back to the Napoleonic wars, and the Shepway local council, very wisely, used it as a tourist attraction. I liked the life-like statues of the navvies and the soldiers, they put along the edge of The Grove, so I wrote a little verse about the canal, and sent it to the local paper.

THE ROYAL MILITARY CANAL

They're here, on guard, the Musket Men,
(With flowerpot hats, like Bill and Ben),
Equipped, all ready for the start
Of campaigns against Bonaparte.

With pick and shovel, you can see
The Navvies, for there used to be
Seven hundred here, to dig a trench,
To foil invasion by the French.

Now rowing boats and ducks are there
While visitors, from Berck-sur-Mer
May fish, and listen to the band,
On slopes like Teletubby Land.

So let's thank those who brought alive
This past historic tale of Hythe,
Enjoy it ! Yes, we really shall,
The Royal Military Canal.

I had hoped to win 'Letter of the week', in 'The Folkestone & Hythe Herald', but absolutely nothing happened!

We had planned our finances fairly carefully since we left York, and, after the sale of Furlong House and four of the cottages, we still had enough to buy something in the area around Hythe, to let, as a booster to our cash flow. Val had become my friend and mentor, so I asked her advice, and she suggested a new build, not too far from Ashford. She even knew of a planned development at Sellinge, that was going to be reasonably priced. They were calling the little terrace, 'The Chestnuts', and there were to be about twenty houses, most of them with two bedrooms. Each house had a patio garden, and they were set around a courtyard parking space, so they wouldn't seem too crowded.

The builders were brothers, called Ken and Kent, who had had a Robin Reliant garage on the plot, and they had taken Val's advice to spend time and money on a really good design for their first ever development. We agreed to buy one after we had seen the plans, as they looked as though they would make comfortable, quite roomy homes. I told Mike and Jan about our new 'cottage' in The Chestnuts, and said we must think of a name. Mike joked that we mustn't call it 'Conkers', so, of course, that's exactly what we did! When the house was ready, I presented the brothers with a painting done by the artist in Allery. It was called 'Les Marrons', and was of a group of lovely shiny conkers against a background of chestnut leaves. 'Conkers', the house, let very easily, but after six months the tenant left to get married, and then, thanks to Val, we sold it at a nice little profit, and hurried back to France to spend it on our renovations there.

Once I realised that we would be spending a lot of time in Picardy, I resigned from drama examining, as it would have been far too expensive to keep popping, to and fro, across the Channel. I had had great fun staying with various friends, who lived near any of the schools on my list. Cliff, at Weybridge, had not been too far from Reading, though I managed to get lost on the journey down the M3. Evelyn, my best friend at the Holy Family Convent, had retired to a village near Burgess Hill, in East Sussex, where I was to examine, so I came down from York and stayed with her, while John, our first Spurs guest, was at Matlock, close to the school in Derby. I had thoroughly enjoyed being a team leader, but now it was time to move on.

Yet another new introduction into the already crowded school year were the SATS tests, aimed at monitoring the progress a child made between ages 7 and 18. The first three points on the age progression were 7, 11 and 14, with O and A level GCE , covering 16 and 18, the end of a school career. The results were published as 'League Tables', supposedly identifying good or failing schools, and caused endless worry to parents choosing a secondary school. It was a political, rather than an educational agenda, inevitably leading to coaching in exam techniques to try to get a good 'score'. I applied to be a marker for English at Key Stage 3, and came down to London, from York, for initiation into the mysteries of the new testing methods. Luckily I had Hilary, who was very bright and enthusiastic, as my team leader, and she made the rather involved marking procedure, crystal clear. I went back to York, ready to get cracking on the first papers, as soon as they arrived.

The exam board used a postal service to carry the finished work from the school to the marker, and everything that could go wrong, went wrong. However, I finally received my allocation, marked them all very carefully, and then sent a selection to Hilary, for her to check that I had kept to the correct standard in awarding marks. There was really no room for deviation if the tests were to have any national validity. It was fairly dull work, requiring real concentration, and a realisation of how important, the result might prove to be, both for the school and for the pupil. The big plus was that it was quite well paid, and it didn't involve travelling. The best thing from my point of view, was meeting Hilary, and her charming husband, Bob, who both became wonderful new bricks in my Wall of Friendship.

Several years later, when I was a team leader, and Hilary was a Senior Marker, I wrote this verse especially for her. Edexcel had been dropped, having failed as the exam's organiser, and the new Board, AQA, was also having problems.

"ASSESSED THE AQA WAY"

The final scripts are marked, so we have finished this
year's Key Stage 3,
We've done our best, and, praise the Lord, we've tried to
satisfy the Board.

Now all of England, so they say, will be assessed the AQA
way,
And, fingers crossed, all will be well. (No muddles, as with
Edexcel!)

Alas, how soon that dream would fade, the training scripts were all delayed,
And changing venues made it clear, we might not meet our teams this year.

We noticed, with a little sigh, how admin tends to multiply,
Whatever's AMI , we say ? And who on earth are QCA?

The script deliveries, of course, relied on good old Parcel Force,
You're out? That fact they just record, then send the scripts back to the Board!

Not 'candidates', but pupils who can't spell, provide a smile or two,
FUNAMENON ECLISPS the sun, the play's Mc BETH, (the Scottish one).

The essay caused a little panic, for someone who had seen 'Titanic',
Described the drowning of a daughter, entitled simply, 'DEAF BY WATER'.

But now the final checks are through, (I didn't lose that twenty-two!)
Reports are written, and one may fill in the hard-earned claims for pay.

Away with biros, red or green, no stacks of scripts can now be seen.
And things have changed. You wonder why? My thumb's developed RSI!

It really had. I had marked over a thousand scripts and I had to go to the osteopath for treatment.

Toffee had come for tea at our new house in Hythe, and it was sad to see that she obviously had considerable health problems. She was unsteady on her feet, and had difficulty getting up to the sitting room on the first floor. She was, however, cheerful and optimistic, and I planned to take her on a day visit to France, to see 'Les Rosiers', as soon as the weather got warmer. I was determined to try to improve her quality of life, which, though she was financially very well off, looked pretty poor. She was, by far, the youngest of four sisters, and had spent her life helping to look after the other three when they got old. It was, definitely, her turn to have some fun.

The meetings called by AQA, took place in various cities, and in 2003, we all went up to Newcastle. I had been there on theatre trips from York, as the RSC often transferred plays to the Theatre Royal from Stratford, and that was certainly much too good to miss. For the SATS discussions, we stayed for two days, so it was interesting to look round the area. We went in a little group to Gateshead, and saw the 'Eye' bridge open and close, and ate at a bistro by the Tyne. While we were chatting in our hotel, one of the markers asked if anyone was interested in buying a pedigree border collie puppy, as she had three for sale. For some reason, my name came up as a possible customer, but I was keen to explain that, sadly, much as I would love to have one, we lived on the Kent coast, and it would not be possible for me to take one back, all that way, on the train. She was, to my surprise, delighted. It turned out that she lived just two miles from Folkestone, at Hawkinge, where she bred collies, so when could I come and see them? I took Paul there the following week, and, to keep Jacques company, we chose a friendly little ball of black and white fur, and Paul named him, Jim.

The more I thought about the key stage 3 English test, the more doubtful I became about its educational value. I contacted the Hythe MP, and asked him to find out exactly how much it cost, to run this part of the exam. The answer stunned me, as it came to about £13,000,000, money that I felt had been totally wasted. Worse still, the letter, in response to his enquiry, actually said, 'It is ONLY costing thirteen million," I really felt that I should stop doing the marking, in protest against this ridiculous misuse of pupils' time and public funds, so I wrote to the Board, resigning as a team leader, withdrawing from the marking, and saying exactly why. Did that sink the SATS ship? It didn't even rock the boat!

The whole idea of buying 'Les Rosiers', was to live there for reasonably long periods of time, and get the 'Right In France' consultancy started. Once we had the Hythe house up and running, we packed our bags, took the dogs and the Sky TV box, and went through the tunnel, to Allery. The journey was under three hours, door to door, which made return visits to Hythe reasonably painless, though the dogs could not go back to England for several months, when their pet passports would become valid.

When we saw the garden at 'Les Rosiers', full of flowers in the summer sun, we were amazed at what our money had bought us in France. The house had been owned by the manager of the jute factory, and the barn had been used for drying the plant before it was processed. Apparently, the whole area had been very prosperous because of this trade, and there was even a little disused railway line, which had once carried jute products from the three factories in Allery. When the trade collapsed, with the advent of man-made fibres, so did the general prosperity of this part of the Somme valley. The little general store opposite our house was the only shop remaining in a village that had once had three butchers.

Philip, our architect, had got the work started on the refurbishment of the maison d'amis. He had engaged a craftsman joiner, who reminded me of 'Big Ears' in the Noddy books. He was a meticulous worker, never looking for a quick solution to any problem, and we could tell that the job would last for several months. He was also a locksmith, and frequently disappeared from his work with us, to help the police by opening, or replacing, doors and locks. The Boyz had started work in the house while we were away, and Paul's room and my en-suite bathroom were ready to use, and looked wonderful. The conservatory, leading straight out of the kitchen, had been finished, and furnished with the obligatory wicker sofa and chairs, and the same glass firm had replaced the veranda windows with double glazed, sliding panels. It was all go!

Paul soon got to know a lot of people in Allery, and found that many of the older villagers spoke a slightly bastardised version of French, called 'picard', that he found almost impossible to understand. I soon realised that my studies with Alliance Français, had not quite prepared me for social chatting in rural Picardy, and made do with cheerful 'bonjours', whenever I passed anyone in the street. Paul was a welcome recruit to the village band, which had a tuba, but no-one who could play it, and he went, dutifully, to long practices for the occasional public performance.

'The Telethon', an annual fund-raising event in France, gave him a chance to get really involved with the community at large, and before you could say knife, or even 'couteau', he knew everyone, and everyone knew him. It would not be easy for a six foot five Englishman, to pass unrecognised, in a village in northern France, where the average height must be about a foot shorter. Very soon he was on the equivalent of the parish council, and generously gave both time and money to every local activity. He wanted us to be a real part of the village, not just two English people who owned that house opposite the shop.

After a while we were introduced to Bernadette, who was the Scrabble champion of Picardy, and played the organ at the 14th century church. Paul gave me a dreadful fright when he, mischievously, convinced her that I was an excellent pianist, and could easily stand in for her at Sunday morning mass. Since my repertoire consisted of the first few bars of Grieg's 'Morning', plus a simplified version of 'Melody in F', I was horrified when she took his remarks seriously. She thought my protests were driven by natural modesty rather than complete ineptitude, and was genuinely disappointed when she finally realised that she was back on her own at the church organ. I had asked her how she knew when to start any particular piece, and she explained that Sylvie would tap her shoulder at the right moment. When we watched this happen, we ended up in hysterics, as, each time, Sylvie gave her such a hard shove, that she nearly fell off the organ stool!

We started having fairly regular Scrabble sessions with Bernadette, and, as I had noticed when I looked for a rhyme, French made the game quite easy. Always assuming that you knew the word in the first place, the endings of the regular verbs, adjectives and adverbs, could often be added, to make impressive scores.

At the Bridge Club, every Tuesday afternoon, some very elegant, charming men, like Marc and Jean-Pierre, caught my eye, as well as several interesting women, intelligent and amusing, but talking to them was hard work as I could never remember the right words. I had hoped to take some French lessons, but as we could not find any classes, even at the Jules Verne University in Amiens, I contented myself with trying to read the 'Courier Picard' each morning. It specialised in dull, static pictures of cycling teams and local murder victims, under baffling headlines, so in the end, I abandoned even that pretence, and we had the overseas 'Times', delivered every day, to the shop across the road!

Having an English newspaper may not have helped my mastery of French, but it kept me up to date in what was going on in the big wide world, outside Picardy. The Courier Picard had just two pages of news headed 'La Monde', and that space had to cover the entire world, for that day. Even news of events in the rest of France was given very little coverage, and I supposed that the villagers got their information from television news programmes. Or maybe it didn't really matter if it was anything outside the boundaries of their little world?

I had always had a layman's doubts about the value of 'modern art', and when the The Times relayed the news that the Turner Prize had been won by the construction of a shed, from a boat, that had once been a shed, it merely confirmed my worst fears. I couldn't resist a celebration in rhyme.

THE TURNER PRIZE 2005

It really comes as no surprise
To hear what won the Turner Prize.
We'd always guessed, it must be said,
The winner would be 'Shed-Boat-Shed'.

Though fuddy-duddies make the point
That judging might be out of joint,
Yet, who are we, who would decry
The triumph here of D.I.Y?

A new approach, will always show
The light, (to persons in the know),
So how could anyone refuse
To empathise with wayout views?

One idea they'd already tried
Was 'Something-in-Formaldehyde',
Another year, it must be said,
The winner was 'An-Unmade-Bed'.

The cognicenti make it clear
No simple paintings can appear
In winning lists. Why, for a start,
How could one call them 'Modern' art?

So, forward march! (And, never fear,
They'll do the same again next year.)
The Turner prize must 'educate'
The public, through the Modern Tate !

Several times, in Paris, when we went around the Quai D'Orsay, and looked at the superb work of the Impressionists. It was difficult to believe that they were the new face of art, in their day. The skill and imaginative flair that the paintings showed was breath-taking, and we wondered what had happened to the art world, that such talent should be replaced by the pedestrian dreariness of beds and sheds. It was reasonably easy to go from Amiens to Paris for the day, and Richard suggested that we should make up our minds to go there on a regular basis. He was quite right, for it is all too easy to talk about making the trip, and very rarely actually doing it.

We very much liked 'La Coupole', an art deco brasserie, that seated about four hundred diners. We were there with Jan and Mike one August day, and Jan and I had just gone to the ladies room, for a wash and brush up. As I stood waiting for Jan, a woman came in through the door. She gave an exclamation of surprise. "Mrs Norris ! Fancy seeing you!" I had no idea who she was, but it turned out that I had taught her in Cheshunt. It seemed a huge coincidence, as she was only in Paris for a day, and the chance of meeting her ex-teacher was several millions to one, especially as, if she had come to the cloakroom twenty seconds later, we would have gone back to our table.

An even stranger happening was on Paul's birthday, when we had gone for lunch at 'Les Ambassadeurs', the smartest venue in Paris. Again Jan and I were washing our hands after a morning's sight-seeing, when, into the washroom came a smartly dressed woman, who looked exactly like Karen. I was so taken with the similarity that I whispered to Jan, to look and see if she agreed. Jan greeted the newcomer with a hug. It really was Karen! Paul had kept it secret that she and James, who I thought were in London, were joining us in Paris for lunch.

'Right In France' had made a fairly slow start, as Paul was involved with so much else, but gradually, through his website, he was contacted by several people with queries about property in our area. Quite often they would have a totally unrealistic idea of the cost of buying a house in northern France, expecting to pay about £50,000 for a detached cottage with a big garden and a sea view, and Paul would have to break the news that it might well be at least five times that amount. However, in time, he had considerable success, including playing a part in selling a delightfully spacious house to the cousin of the poet laureate, and being able to restore peace of mind to an Australian, who had acquired several chateaux, but was totally baffled by the French tax system.

One very pleasant young couple, rang to thank Paul for his help, and told him that they had decided to buy a house in a new development at Merlimont, which was next door to the prestigious resort of Le Touquet. It sounded so good that we drove over to see it for ourselves. On the agent's model, the new development looked very attractive, backing on to the sand dunes that led down to the sea. The houses, mostly with two bedrooms, had first floor balconies, and little front and back gardens, but we could see from the floor plans that they were rather small inside. The front door opened straight into the main living room, which took up the whole of the ground floor, with a tiny kitchen, and to our surprise, the only lavatory. Up some stairs from this room, were two bedrooms, one with the balcony, and a family bathroom with a bath and a wash basin. It was a real 'holiday home', rather than a house for a family to live in.

We had a long talk with the agent and decided to reserve one, which we would let to tourists, and drove back to Allery to plan the alterations we would make to the design. By the time we were home we had settled on a name, 'Happy Days', which we felt would suit the English clients and not be too difficult for everyone else. We spoke to The Boyz, hoping they could move the lavatory upstairs, into the bathroom, and they agreed to do it. We were all puzzled as to why it wasn't there in the first place.

Once the building work and the alterations were finished, I got to play my 'Dolls House' game and we chose furniture and china and linen and so on, till it had become a comfortable holiday home for those happy days. Jan and Mike came to stay in Allery and raised money for the linen by taking a stall at the Allery 'rederie', and selling a variety of things they had brought from England. The tools went very quickly, but the books in English were less popular! Paul had agreed to do the 'turn round' every Saturday, so we contacted an agent and put 'Happy Days' on the holiday market, where it proved to be extremely popular.

All the guests were English, and Merlimont was a perfect little seaside town for visitors. Every Saturday, Paul made the hundred mile round trip to get the house ready for the next family, and though he never complained, I thought it was a terrible waste of his time, and that we should find a domestic to do the chores. As it happened, after a year, we decided to sell 'Happy Days' and use the money to rebuild our ruined barn, which was much less stressful and considerably nearer home.

Chapter 22

To find a name for the new project, I looked up the words for 'the barn' in the French/ English dictionary, and the name was there, ready-made, 'La Grange', so we looked no further. Philip designed a wonderfully exciting building and we managed to get the go-ahead from the authorities. The old wooden cruck-construction skeleton, grew into an elegant leisure complex. The wide pine staircase led from the entrance hall to a beautifully spacious open area, with French doors on to a balcony, overlooking the garden. I had my Clavinola, that looked like a piano, and an easel with water colour paints and drawing paper, just in case I ever discovered that I had any artistic talent. It seemed unlikely, but probably Grandma Moses's family were amazed when she became an artist at ninety.

La Grange had two double bedrooms and a study, plus a huge bathroom, with a walk-in shower. The really amazing thing, however was the tree. Right beside the staircase, in the entrance hall, we planted a magnolia grandiflora, which had rubber-plant-like evergreen leaves. Its roots went down into the subsoil, and it grew so quickly that it had nearly reached the roof when we left France. A visit to Ikea in Lille, solved our furnishing problems, and I resolved to learn to paint at the earliest opportunity. We put in a sink, an electric hob and a little fridge, in case someone wanted to do some cooking, and we even had an opening ceremony to start the ball rolling.

It happened that Cliff and John were driving to Portugal, across France and Spain, and with a little deviation, could call in at Les Rosiers. Jan and Mike, plus Penny and Diana from Bramcote, were staying with us, and we invited Philip with his wife and son, to come along for a barbeque lunch. We fixed a ribbon across the front door of La Grange, which was nearly finished, and Cliff did a splendidly formal, "I now declare this barn open!" By a lucky chance, Tommy and Carole, our English friends from the village, came by to replace a bottle of milk we had given them, and Carole, who had been a Cliff fan from the earliest days, thought she was hallucinating when she saw the star of so many shows, in our garden!

In England, the French Property Show, at Olympia, was attracting crowds of potential buyers and soon became an annual promotional opportunity for 'Right In France'. Paul would hire a unit, like a very small office, with wall space to display pictures of attractive properties, and a desk, with three chairs, for chats with prospective clients. I played 'keep-net', and if he was talking to someone, I would try to keep them on ice, till he was free. On the whole that worked well, and we would stay in a nearby hotel each night, to be ready to start work the next day. It was quite an expensive exercise, but it often produced reasonably successful results.

Most of Paul's properties were in villages some distance from Allery, but, inevitably, there were some in the village itself. Tommy and Carole, the really sparky couple from Liverpool, had moved into a house just the other side of the war memorial, and Carole and I went to yoga classes together. I saw that, with her legs flat on the floor, she could bend forward and put her head on her knees, which was tremendously impressive. My head and knees remained a considerable distance apart, despite strenuous efforts to bring them together. A big house, on the same road as 'Les Rosiers', was bought by two chaps from London, and there was another Englishman, married to a local artist, living on the other side of the old jute warehouse. In all, there were seven English people in Allery, and I wondered how the locals would feel, if the number increased still further. A wild rabbit in our garden, eating my carefully planted annuals, gave me the idea, and I couldn't resist writing about the possibility of future resentment of the English 'invaders'.

THE RABBIT

Unexpectedly, today, there is a rabbit in our garden,
Silently nibbling its way through the flower beds.
It had a special penchant for French marigolds.
Now the marigolds have all gone, and it has begun
To eat the white petunias. It makes an interesting topic
Of conversation. We wish it well. One little bunny.

We wonder what would happen, if another rabbit
Came to join it? Before long there might be a family
Of little bunnies, quietly munching their way
Through the geraniums, and the busy lizzies,
Till only the bare earth was left for us. We would
Have to make them feel unwelcome. One way or another.

Unexpectedly, today, there are strangers in our village,
Silently unsettling the status quo. We can't understand
What they say. They really seem quite different from us,
But now they're here, so can it ever be the same again?
Or is it that the things we care about are changing,
Disappearing overnight, like the French marigolds?

In fairness to Allery, I must say that people were always pleasant and polite. However, after all the generous efforts Paul had made to be a part of the community, I thought it was interesting that, when we left after eight years, no-one came to say goodbye, and, for the record, even the rabbit disappeared. The Bridge Club , however, gave us a wonderful send-off, with champagne, valedictory speeches and the presentation of a beautiful bouquet, but that was in Amiens, not in a village. Of course we had had a lot of English friends to stay for a few days, and at times it must have looked to the villagers as though we were working up to a replay of the battle of Crécy, which was, by coincidence, only a few kilometres away.

James and Karen and the Grils had stayed in the house, before the renovation work had started, so they were able to see a big improvement every time they came. Charlie with Jan and Mike, and Giles with Ali, were wonderful guests and we really missed them when they left. When Derek visited, we explored all the restaurants around, but Picardy is not noted for its haute cuisine, so, though we had several quite good meals, there was nothing that either he or Paul couldn't have done, just as well, at home. For one July 14th, my central friend, John came all the way from Ireland, bringing with him, Mary, a fascinating ex-nun, with a great sense of humour, who worked in the community as a physiotherapist. I'd often wondered what it felt like to have those little needles stuck in you, and she put several in my arm, just to prove they didn't hurt at all. Irish voices filled the house with the delightful sounds of joy and laughter, and the place seemed empty for several days after they had gone. I brought Toffee on that day trip I had planned, and when Nigel and Nicky, two of my favourite guests came to stay, we did a tour of the Somme battlefields, where one of his family friends had been killed. On the huge memorial arch at Thiepval, we searched the heart-breaking list of the names of those whose bodies were never found, until we identified the right one.

Along with many other schools, Bramcote had been taking pupils on tours of the battlefields for many years, and Richard and Paul, with John, the head of history, had all been involved in leading school parties to the Somme. It seemed perfectly natural that, once we had a large house nearby, we should play host to Bramcote on these visits. The group usually came in early June, and I would disappear back to England, so that they could have the use of my bedroom, and I could finish my key stage 3 marking in peace and quiet.

We did have quite a lot of space at Les Rosiers, as the big family bedroom in the maison d'amis, made a good dormitory, La Grange had the benefit of three bedrooms and the large sitting area, while the main house had three more bedrooms and Paul's extensive study. As well as all that, there was lots of room for table tennis and other games in the garden, or on the paved courtyard, and we would get a portable plastic swimming pool for everyone to splash around in. Every year, 'Bramcote arrive' and 'Bramcote leave' were entered on the diary as key fixtures, and Paul really looked forward to seeing them all in France. The village youths soon discovered that a bevy of very attractive girls had landed in their laps, and they hung around the big courtyard gates, hoping for a glimpse of this forbidden fruit. Several parents came, too, and a chateau just about a mile away, provided B&B, and a rest from the exhausting group dynamics, inseparable from any gathering of energetic teenagers.

One year was especially interesting, because, when the group arrived at the Thiepval Monument, they found a television crew, with the veteran commentator, Charles Wheeler, making a series of short inserts for the ten o'clock news, about the imminent anniversary of the Battle of the Somme. He asked for permission to film the Bramcote party, and the staff were fascinated, to watch the techniques he used to get the children to relax, and say, quite naturally, what they thought of the experience. He would do the regular interview, just as they expected, with the camera and the microphone very much in evidence, and the resulting rather pat answers to questions, being offered in very self-conscious voices. That over, he would sit down and chat about how they really felt, and then, relaxed and confident, they would give him the interview he would use in the television programme. The Headmaster was immensely pleased with the result when it was broadcast, as it was excellent sales promotion for this very good prep school.

Back in Hythe, tending my damaged thumb and the resultant marking problems, I began to wonder if we really needed a house, rather than a flat, as our pied-a-terre. When I casually mentioned the idea to James, I was amazed at his reaction. He thought we should not sell the house, as Hythe was an ideal holiday town, and they all liked it tremendously. I told Janice, and it seemed that she thought the same. Her grandchildren, Harry and Maisie, had learnt to ride their bikes on The Grove, and had been fascinated by watching the fishermen on the beach. They had loved the children's playground at the bottom of the cliff, and being taken, by Mike, on the Military Canal in a rowing boat. I could see it was not going to be a popular move.

Paul thought differently, and it turned out that he had grave reservations about the size of the bedrooms and the general pokiness of newly-built houses. We decided to see what kind of flats were available, and how much they cost, so we went to Folkestone and did a sweep down the main street, calling in at every estate agency. The most effective way for us to search was to separate, and each take one side of the Sandgate Road, which has a plethora of agencies. It was difficult to see how so many could make a living, and there must be a lot of moving from here to there, as they all seemed to be reasonably prosperous.

My side of the road started with 'Hunters', and I immediately struck, what looked like gold. Charm has to be the agent's best weapon in the selling war, and David had it in spades. I explained that we were living, much of the time, in France, and that we felt a flat might be a better English base than a house. He completely agreed, and told me that, by chance, he had just the flat for us. It took up the whole ground floor of a large Victorian house, near the shops and the Leas, and it had its own garage, which was, he said, very unusual in Folkestone. It had only just come on the market, and he thought it would sell very quickly. We should look at it pronto! It was only just round a couple of corners from the agency, and he would arrange a viewing for the next day. David gave his most charming smile. He could tell that he had made a good impression on me, and he was right.

Paul had had a less successful journey down the other side of the high street, so he was very pleased that there was a possible runner in our 'flat race'. We drove round to look at the outside of the building and we were impressed. It was a really elegant mid-Victorian house, and the windows on the ground floor looked huge, so the flat must be very light. The road was a real avenue, with traffic going down either side of a tree-lined central reservation, and turning through roundabouts at each intersection. The top of the cliffs was a short walk away, and around the corner opposite the house, there was a little supermarket. The garage looked substantial, and there was a balcony running along the length of the ground floor, so we were pleased with our initial impression. We went round the next day, and the owners were very pleasant. He had just retired from the army and they were going to move to Lincoln, as soon as they sold the flat.

It was just what we wanted, so, silently thanking that guardian angel for yet another success, we explained that we had not yet put our Hythe house on the market, but we were fairly sure it would sell quite quickly. The lovely spacious hall, the elegant drawing room and the two huge bedrooms, delighted Paul, though we both thought that the galley kitchen and the house bathroom would both need a face lift. At the back there was a room that had made a good study, with a door into what they called a sun room and I thought looked like a rather tacky lean-to. The dining area between the kitchen and the drawing room, had a door out onto the front balcony, and behind the property, stretched the green grass and trees of Augusta Gardens. The price was about thirty thousand less than we expected to get for the Hythe house, so that would cover the alterations we could see were needed. We told them we were very interested and hurried back to arrange the sale of 'Wellington House'.

The always tedious process of selling a house went through reasonably quickly, as we were experienced veterans now, ready to sort out any disasters as they came. It seemed no time at all before our furniture was in the moving van outside, and the house was empty. I breathed a sigh of relief and said to Paul, "Well, that's it, nothing can go wrong now!" I had, foolishly tempted fate, and so, the telephone rang. It was our friend, Nigel, with his solicitor's hat on, who suggested that I should sit down. Apparently, our chain had fractured at the bottom, so no-one could go ahead. The first buyer had failed to lodge the money in the bank, and it was Friday, so we would have to wait till the weekend was over, before we could move.

I could not believe it. So near, and yet so far. I asked Nigel why we couldn't go into the flat and pay on Monday, but he assured me that that was not on the cards. It was like "No pain, no gain!", no money, no move. He promised to have one last try to mend the broken link, but he didn't hold out much hope. By the time the phone rang again, ten minutes later, we already had a plan to put the dogs into kennels, and spend the weekend in the Imperial Hotel in Hythe, sipping champagne cocktails. Nigel's voice was triumphant. He had told off the offending solicitor so strongly that they had made one final effort to lodge the vital cheque, and the deal was done. I thanked him from the bottom of my heart, and rushed out to give the go-ahead to the moving men, who sped off, like wagons in the wild west. We put the dogs into the car, and followed, to take up residence in the best flat in Folkestone, and, at this moment, we're still there.

Chapter 23

Since our move to France, in 2001, we had enjoyed some wonderful holidays, here, there, and everywhere. Paul had really loved Kerala, in the south of India, where he played cricket with the local boys beside the beach, and in 2006, I persuaded him to try cruising on Cunard's Queen Mary2, on the round trip to my beloved New York. It was great fun, and we were especially impressed by the Captain, who ran the ship brilliantly, and who had, I immediately noted, lovely blue eyes. Paul discovered that Bernard was from North Yorkshire, and had gone to one of the prep schools that Bramcote played in games of rugby and cricket. They got on well, and we were given the accolade of an invitation to dine at the Captain's Table, on the return voyage to Southampton. I was thrilled to bits, and even went to the Beauty Spa to have my hair shampooed specially for the occasion.

When, that evening, we arrived at the superbly decorated round table, my name was on a place-card, next to the Captain. I was so glad I'd had my hair done! Bernard looked superb in his formal uniform, with a short cut jacket, dazzlingly white evening shirt, black bow-tie and masses of gold buttons and gold braid. All the other guests were suitably smartly dressed, and I was conscious that my outfit fell very far short of haute couture. Once the Captain was seated, a photographer appeared to record the event for posterity, and when I saw the picture the next day, I thought I looked as though I was about to slip under the table.

The conversation, on such occasions, is always slightly awkward. What does one say to the Captain, that he hasn't heard hundreds of times before? I had crossed the Atlantic in 1948, on the original Queen

Elizabeth, but I certainly didn't want to mention that. Nearly fifty years later, it made me seem well past my prime! I fell back on an obvious question, that put the ball in his court. We had been to New York: where else did the ship go? When he told me it went to Barbados, I thought of Cliff, who had had a house built there several years before, so I said, "I've got a friend with a villa in Barbados!", and he promptly answered, "So has Tony Blair!" I just couldn't resist saying, "It's the same friend!".

Very luckily, Cliff was giving a concert in Birmingham, later in the year when Bernard was home on leave, and as he lived in Warwickshire, he was able to bring his attractive wife Tina, and some friends, to see the show. Cliff joined us afterwards in a Chinese restaurant, and we all had a wonderful evening.

Not content with one cruise, I very much wanted to go again on the QM2, this time to Barbados. Charlie, who had heard all our stories of the wonders of the Captain's Table, and had met Bernard at the concert, decided to join us, but soon discovered that there were no single cabins on the ship. The cost, for one person, was almost the same as it was for two, so very kindly, he gave an actor friend, a free cruise to the Caribbean.

I told Cliff we were coming to Bridgetown, and would love to see him, and he responded as generously as ever, and invited us all to lunch on the day the ship docked. Bernard was able to join us later, so, after we had done a taxi tour of the island, we picked him up at the dock, and we all went together to see the new villa. It was superb, beautifully secluded, with a glorious garden and a really breathtaking view, from the pool, out to sea. The house had space and charm, and it was every bit as wonderful as we had thought it would be. John had organised a delicious lunch, which we ate in the gazebo by the pool.

Looking out to sea, I joked that it would be great fun if the QM2 could sail close by, Cliff could then flash a light from the house, and, maybe the ship could flash back in response. Cliff said he had just the right kind of light for the job, if only the ship was close enough. To everyone's surprise, Bernard thought it might be possible to change course, and sail past the villa, so Cliff should be ready to signal by about seven o'clock that evening, and he cheerfully promised he would be.

The others decided to take a taxi to the fabulous hotel at Sandy Lane for a quick, and very expensive drink, and John and Cliff drove Bernard and me back to the QM2, and were given a VIP tour of this beautifully appointed ocean liner. They said goodbye, and hurried back to the villa to get the flash equipment ready, just in case it was needed. To my amazement, Bernard was not joking, and promptly set about making a slight change in the course the ship would take after she had left the harbour at Bridgetown. We were invited to join him on the bridge to see the fun.

I don't think that I shall ever forget the moment when Cliff's flashing light was spotted in the distance and Bernard leant forward and gave the order to switch on the floodlights on the ship. We were dazzled as the huge foredeck blazed with light, and then flashed on and off twice more. The Captain of a ship was, certainly, a very powerful man! Paul got the villa on his mobile phone and reported that Cliff was nearly speechless with excitement.

This was, indeed, just the beginning of an almost unbelievable saga. Every time the Queen Mary went to Barbados that winter, the flashing light exchange was repeated, with the ship slowing down as she lit up, and the Captain telling the excited fans on board, who was being greeted. Cliff was so thrilled that, as a surprise thank you, he brought a firework expert over from Canada, and when the ship flashed her lights, the response was an impressive display of fireworks. I was delighted to have had a part in this marvellous game.

Without doubt, Queen Mary 2 is our favourite ship, Bernard our favourite captain, (now promoted to Commodore!), and Cunard our favourite cruising line. You just can't go wrong with such a trio of winners, and, naturally, I wrote a little verse to celebrate all the fun we had on board.

WHY NOT GO ON A CRUISE?

Want some fun? Why not go on a cruise?
(And Queen Mary's the ship you should choose),
There's that peach of a Captain, warm tones he employs
And his clear blue eyes sparkle with evident joys,
But he's talking about his sweet wife and the boys!
Watch your heart, when you go on a cruise,
For it's so very easy to lose!

Things can change as you lie in the sun,
(Well, the depth of your wrinkles is one!)
Get a moderate tan. That might well have been said
In the notes, on those warnings you ought to have read,
But, alas, it's too late when you've gone beetroot red!
So get into the shade when you're 'done'.
For a burn on your back, isn't fun!

Wonder who might your table-mates be?
'So delightful', or just, 'not for me'?
There's a type ,with loud voices, who're dying to tell
Of the cruising they've done, and you know very well,
That you're longing to say "Why not just go to hell ?"
Change of table? No problem, for see,
It's the freedom to move that's the key!

There are lifts when you're touring the ship,
Just in case you have fractured your hip,
And the staff are so helpful, they'll all take a share,
They will guard you from harm and they do seem to care,
But it's hard to seem young, with those wheels on your chair!
As you'll see when you've taken a trip
And beware, it's so easy to slip!

All the staterooms are terribly grand,
From the suites to the much-lower band,
If a stay in a 'Queen' is unlikely for you,
For that needs all your lottery dreams to come true,
Then just welcome a porthole with light shining through,
So you'll see when the ship's nearing land,
And there might be a welcoming band!

To those halcyon days, it's goodbye!
To the sailors I've loved I must cry,
"Don't forget me, although you are sailing away,
I shall miss you, so, thank you, is all I can say,
May your journeys be safe, and be happy each day,
Till we meet, once again, you and I,
For it's just au revoir, not goodbye!"

Our eight year stay in France, came to a rather abrupt end, when Paul spotted surveyors working on the field next to the house. On enquiry, it turned out that the land had been sold to a developer for the building of a small estate of 'Les Pavillons', that least attractive of all modern French houses. They are, however, very popular with young couples or older retired people, as they are easy to run, have all mod cons, and are, above all, cheap to buy. They sold easily, and developers were jumping on the band wagon of pavillons, wherever they could get planning consent. These little houses, always appeared to us to be a cross between a pre-fab and a 1930's seaside bungalow, and large numbers had been built in our area, so we knew just what to expect. Paul felt that we should sell-up and go back to England, before building started.

We were sure that the estate agents would set a reasonably attractive price on Les Rosiers, so we invited several round to come up with a figure that we could accept. They were all duly impressed, as the property was made up of three separate units, the main house, the Maison d'Amis and La Grange, and we had spent a great deal of money on paving the huge courtyard at the side of the house, with attractive six inch squares of coloured tiles. We had tried to make everything just right for us, and there were fruit trees, a small fish pond, and large, well-groomed lawns, cut regularly by Paul, on the sit-on mower.

The first disappointment was that, because inland villages in Picardy are not sought-after locations for French buyers, we were going to be pushed to get our money back. For the first time in my property deals, there was very little chance of making a profit. I recognised that this was my fault, as when I had an idea for a new renovation extravaganza, the cost had never been an issue. There was always something we could sell, to pay the bill. I worked out that, had we stayed in Furlong House in York, and kept the five cottages we had bought there, we would have been millionaires, but then, think of the fun we'd had, moving around!

After several false alarms, when we thought we had sold Les Rosiers to excited English couples, we reduced the asking price by a massive hundred thousand euros. Almost at once we had two firm offers from clients with different agents. It became a question of who would act first. One agent, almost immediately, asked us to meet her clients in the firm's Amiens office, to sign the 'compromis de vente', which sets the whole legal process in motion. This was a particularly important point in the sale, as the buyers had to put down a non-returnable deposit of ten percent of the purchase price. Accordingly, we arrived in Amiens, cock-a-hoop that, after an unexpectedly long wait, the sale of Les Rosiers would go through.

Within the first minute, we realised there were problems. The couple wanted to set some totally unacceptable clauses into the agreement. If they had difficulty selling their house in Amiens, they would not be able to complete the purchase of Les Rosiers, and, moreover, would expect their deposit to be returned. There was absolutely no way we could agree to this scenario, so we thanked the agent, shook everyone's hand, and, very disappointed, drove back to Allery. Very fortunately, the other agent had not advised his clients that they had lost the house, and within days, delightful Monsieur and Madame Leon Bayard had put down the deposit, and the sale was completed three months later.

On the day of the handover, they arrived to collect the keys, carrying the largest basket of delicious fruit I had ever seen. We had left a bottle of champagne ready for them, and they seemed very thrilled to have bought such a lovely house. Our great moving man, Chris, had sent a van the day before, to take our stuff to the flat in Folkestone, so all we had to do was say goodbye, put the dogs into the car, and get to the Tunnel.

There was one last hitch, however, for when we got to Calais the woman on duty at the Pet Passport Office, was doing a 'jobsworth'. She queried every past entry by the vet in Oisemont, she questioned the dates of previous anti-rabies injections in England, and she wondered why Jacques had two microchip numbers. Not content with all that, she suggested that it might not be possible for them to return to the UK, until all these matters had been clarified.

Paul had taken the dogs into the Pet Passport office on his own, but I could see him through the big glass window, and his body language told me that he was getting very annoyed. His arms were flailing around in the air, and his head was shaking vigorously, but suddenly that stopped and he briskly came back to the car with Jacques and Jim. He was furious and had quite expected that we would have had to stay in Calais till the next day, to continue the interrogation. Several unrepeatable English phrases, described the lady in question, and we drove away quickly, with Paul protesting that he would never again bring the dogs to France. Funnily enough, there had been a real error on the form, that she didn't spot, which would have invalidated the passports. One of the vets in France had put the wrong date!

Back in England, the flat had changed considerably. The Boyz had stayed in it and we asked them what they would do about the kitchen and the bathroom, if it was their flat. The ideas they offered were, as always, brilliant, and we immediately got, Alan, our English builder, to make the considerable alterations. We now had a wonderfully extended new kitchen and, just off the main hall, a lovely jacuzzi bathroom. The new conservatory was a restful place to sit and read, and we had plans to put a guest room over the garage. I was making the same mistake of investing more than we could possibly get back, but we had created a super place to live.

We had not, actually, lost money on the house in France, for though it looked as though we would get much less back than we had spent, a change in the foreign currency market came to our aid. The euro had been worth about eighty pence, but a sudden rise in the exchange rate, meant that we would receive a much increased return for our French currency. Now we had money to re-invest in property in England, and the question was, what should we buy? The housing market had been affected by the recession, so that to buy, renovate, then sell at a profit, was no longer sure to bring a good result. We had had 'Conkers' at Sellinge, but I really didn't want to be involved in a longer let again. In York, we had had several successful holiday cottages, and I thought that would be more profitable and much more interesting. We could make the place really smart, put in Broadband and a telephone connection, and stay in it ourselves when it wasn't let to holidaymakers.

The next problem was where to look for the right house? I liked the idea of a country retreat on Romney Marsh, a wonderfully unspoilt area with little villages whose names sounded really romantic, like St Mary in the Marsh and Ivychurch. Otherwise, there was New Romney, a delightful little country town, bustling with life, and the nearby holiday resort of Dymchurch, very touristy, but popular with families, as it had a glorious sandy beach. Then two seaside places, Littlestone and Greatstone were worth considering, and even the wilderness around Dungeness. Paul and I did our sweep around the house agents in New Romney, leaving our name and explaining that we were looking for a cottage to let to visitors, and went back home to await results.

After the great fondness for Hythe, Folkestone was proving surprisingly successful as a replacement. James and Karen, with the Grils, came to the flat and loved it, and everyone agreed that it was considerably more elegant, and much larger, than Wellington House. The town also had some very good shops, like Debenham's, but, of course, I kept my invaluable hairdresser in Hythe, now the owner of her own 'Salon 13'. Folkestone had a railway station, with fairly frequent trains to Charing Cross, plus the benefit of a fast service to St Pancras, so an evening at the theatre in London, was very easily arranged.

In Folkestone, I had discovered, almost by accident, a really good doctor. On leaving Hythe, I had had to register with a new GP, so I looked down the list in yellow pages, and there, in a seaside town, was a name that caught my eye, Doctor Beach. I had always been told that sea air was good for you, and the phrase 'Doctor Brighton', had made that town seem a good place to visit if you had been ill. I phoned the surgery, and asked to join the practice list. The following week I saw the nurse, who duly weighed me and checked my blood pressure, tested my urine specimen, and patted me on the back for having given up smoking in 1985.

But I did not see Doctor Beach; for that, I would have to get something wrong with me, and I planned to avoid that happening. Back in France, I decided to write to him, asking if I might, briefly, meet him at some time, when I was at the flat in Folkestone, as I wanted to put a face to the interesting name. To my delight he wrote back, suggesting that I should make an appointment with the surgery, next time I was in England and he would see me then. I did as he said, and so I met a remarkable man and an excellent doctor, who wins my NHS patient's Oscar for 'the best performance by a GP', by the proverbial mile!

I had told Val about our holiday house search, and she came up with several very good properties. The most interesting was a Grade 2 listed cottage in Dymchurch, so we asked her to arrange a viewing as soon as possible. It was really charming, with pretty little windows, a wavy tiled roof, and good gardens front and back. Inside, we met the very pleasant owner, who lived with his elderly mother and kept two horses in a livery stable nearby. Rather charmingly, he was selling the cottage as he didn't feel that the horses were happy in Dymchurch. I liked him immediately. His old mother was in remarkably good shape, and though she was profoundly deaf, she looked very cheerful. She had very few wrinkles, so Paul suggested I should find out what anti-ageing cream she used. Swallowing the implied insult, I asked her son how old she was. The answer amazed me; she was ninety-eight, and certainly looked twenty years younger, so perhaps I missed an opportunity to find the key to an eternal, non-ageing future.

Unfortunately, though we really liked the cottage, our surveyor friend, Terry, advised us that, it would be fine as long as we didn't plan any structural alterations. It was nearly four hundred years old, and had settled into a state that could last for a long time, perfectly happily. He feared that if we started knocking walls down, as we planned to do, we would upset the equilibrium, and create a lot of problems. Reluctantly, we crossed 'The Bridge Cottage' off our list.

Our house hunting drive in New Romney, suddenly paid dividends, and we were sent particulars of a new-build facing the sea at Littlestone, which was the home of Paul's favourite golf club. It looked delightful, with three floors and a balcony overlooking the beach, outside the first floor bedroom, so we nicknamed it the 'Beach House'. It had been bought as a temporary measure by a builder who wanted to put up his own house, and had expected to make a small profit on the deal. The drop in house prices upset that hope, and it was still not selling. I was very impressed by Steve, the local house agent, who very honestly explained the situation to us, and advised his client to consider, seriously, the offer we subsequently made.

The 'Beach House' was part of a small development of ten houses, facing the sea, that had been planned as holiday cottages, but had been bought as family homes. The whole of the ground floor was either tiled or had laminated flooring, and there was a good sized living room, with French doors opening onto the little front garden, with a wonderful view of 'The Greens' and the beach huts.

The well-equipped kitchen/ dining room, had similar doors onto the back garden, and there was a nice long hall with a downstairs cloakroom. The two first floor bedrooms, each had an en-suite shower room, and the two large rooms on the top floor, shared the house bathroom. It would make the perfect holiday cottage, so Steve negotiated a fair price, and we bought it!

Now it is up and running, with a conservatory, which gives a lot of added space to the kitchen, and colourful shrubs in the landscaped, Indian sandstone terraced garden planted by Toby and Sarah. The summerhouse has a quarter size snooker table, which converts into one for table tennis, and an exercise bike and a rowing machine to keep off the extra pounds, that a holiday can so easily add. There is unlimited wireless Broadband, so that guests can keep in touch with goings on, in either business or pleasure, a large HD television, and a telephone landline. We love staying in The Beach House, and so do the many paying guests that Steve, our favourite agent, finds for us. 'The Clean Team', led by super Maz, keeps the house shining bright, and the talented trio of Alf, Barnaby, and Matt deal with everything else. It has been a wonderfully successful venture.

Paul has joined the Littlestone Golf Club, and I am, definitely, a 'golf mother', but he thoroughly enjoys each game, and rates the club and his fellow members, as five star. What more could one want?

Epilogue

For the past four months I, too, have been switched-on by an absorbing new relationship, and, like all close affairs, it has taken time to develop. Inevitably, it will fade and I shall be left with just a memory. Moments of wonderful exhilaration, have been followed long periods of deep despair, but that may be the price one pays, when finding out how to relate to a new partner. Night after night, I have sat up with him till the early hours, trying, with little success, to understand his very strange behaviour.

Quite often, things between us have, obviously, not been right. I expect it has usually been my fault, but surely he should take a little of the blame? The fact that he is Japanese, may account for some of our misunderstandings, but though I find his language difficult, if not totally incomprehensible, I hope this will not upset my plans for our future together. All we can to do is trust each other, so that I can begin to comprehend the way he works, and he can give me the help I so desperately need.

I freely admit that, sometimes, I have screamed abuse at him. I have never done this with anyone before, but I have kept thinking of all the other things I could be doing, rather than spending my time trying to foster a close relationship with such an unresponsive partner. However, despite all the frustration, when I have often decided to have nothing more to do with him, I am drawn back by the sheer fascination of the wonderful things he can do. I really want to save what we have created together, and not just switch off completely.

I have written a serenade, to set out our differences, but the sixty-nine thousand words that have passed between us, will always remain a real testimony to the very special enjoyment of the memories we have explored together.

SERENADE TO TOSHIBA

It was said, a thing of beauty is a joy forever more,
So my lovely new Toshiba, surely rates a super score ?
He shines. silver in the sunlight, and his letters are all clear,
And there's lots of lovely numbers that look very pretty here,

Like an arrow, is his cursor, that just dances round his screen,
And he has the cutest squares to tap, that you have ever seen.
His caps can lock, there's shift and space, and even alt control,
With keys marked F, (from one to twelve), that, clearly, play some role.

Ignore these charms, don't be deceived, Toshiba's NOT a friend,
For though you start by loving him, you'll hate him in the end.
He has spiteful little habits that may puzzle you at first,
For you'll think that there is something wrong, you start to fear the worst!

So, perhaps you're not as clever as you've always seemed to be?
Though you drive a car, and write in verse, it's very clear to see
That, to understand Toshiba, takes a different sort of skill,
And the fear it's one you haven't got, can quickly make you ill.

For all you've done is simply sit and turn your partner on,
And you've found the page you're looking for, and nothing has gone wrong
But now that page has split in two, his font has gone quite small,
His screen then starts to narrow down, it drives you up the wall.

The words you typed italicised, have somehow all gone BOLD,
Although you once felt full of life, you're quickly growing old,
For you have put your heart and soul in all you've written there,
So, 'Rubbish in means rubbish out!', just doesn't seem quite fair.

You try to take your hands away, things go from bad to worse,
For, as you look, his screen goes blank, you'd like to scream
and curse,
And if you had a hammer near, you'd hit him very hard,
Or throw him on an open fire and cover him with lard.

Don't worry, for it's only now destruction's in the air.
Tomorrow is another day, so let him know you care.
Quite gently switch the power off, then very firmly state,
"I've loved our walks down Memory Lane..........
IT'S LAPTOPS THAT I HATE!!!!!"

* * * * *

("O BASH IT!" is an anagram of TOSHIBA)